CU00810490

In order to protect the privacy of the people that have submitted stories some names and locations have been left out.

All stories were originally submitted by our audience to ghostsofamerica.com. The stories have been edited by us to better fit this book.

Compiled and edited by: Nina Lautner

Acknowledgements

We would like to thank all those who have submitted their stories to us. These are the people who make our site ghostsofamerica.com and this book possible.

We would also like to thank all the lost souls in these stories. We hope many of them will have found their way by the time this book is published.

CONTENTS

1. Maybe It's Grandma - Athol, Massachusetts - 6
2. Playful And Weird - Fresno, California - 9
3. Edward The Blacksmith - Hyde Park, Vermont - 11
4. Haunted Building On Ackerman Drive - Lodi, CA - 15
5. Evil Eyes - Maple Shade, New Jersey - 18
6. Frank - Spencer, Massachusetts - 20
7. Little Gnome-Like Creature - Camp Lejeune, NC - 22
8. A Girl And Confederate… - Manchester, PA - 25
9. That Old Place 20 Years Ago - Lordsburg, NM - 28
10. Phillip - West Palm Beach, Florida - 30
11. Taking Care Of The Guests - Clifford, PA - 32
12. Screaming Sheila - Eastland, Texas - 34
13. Angry Man - Barberton, Ohio - 36
14. Not Welcome - Fort Wayne, Indiana - 37
15. Bert And Tilly - Stony Point, New York - 38
16. The Neighbor's Mom - Corona, California - 39
17. The Old Victorian Mansion - Lacon, Illinois - 40
18. Former Resident - Martinez, California - 41
19. Cats Could Tell - Lafayette, Colorado - 43
20. Black Mass - Bellingham, Washington - 46
21. No Longer Scared - Warsaw, Indiana - 48
22. Creepy Face - Lake Arrowhead, California - 52
23. Devil's Tree - Port Saint Lucie, Florida - 54
24. At The High Desert Center - Victorville, CA - 55
25. Ghost Cop - Richardson, Texas - 58
26. Not Happy - Martinsburg, West Virginia - 60
27. He Liked Women - Tempe, Arizona - 61
28. She Ran Fast - Irvine, California - 62
29. Hawaiian Warrior - Honokaa, Hawaii - 63
30. Outside The Door - Canyon, Texas - 65
31. Ghost Dog of Esters Road - Irving, Texas - 67
32. An Elderly Lady - Sayre, Pennsylvania - 68
33. There's More to Life - Sugarloaf, California - 70
34. Third Floor - Mackinac Island, Michigan - 72
35. Comes With Cigar Smell - Natick, Massachusetts - 73
36. Check On My Baby - Tickfaw, Louisiana - 74
37. Standing In The Basement - Anderson, Indiana - 75
38. The Lewis Gratz House - Yoncalla, Oregon - 76

39. In Belfaire Trace Subdivision - Dacula, Georgia - 78
40. An Imprint On My Soul - Lakewood, California - 81
41. Buzz's House - Mill Valley, California - 83
42. Sue - Collins, Missouri - 85
43. Mystery Woman - Spokane, Washington - 87
44. Wolf Pen Gap - Mena, Arkansas - 88
45. Energy Perimeters. - Westchester, Illinois - 89
46. A Cowboy In The Hallway - Mission, Texas - 91
47. Jeffie's Still Here - Provo, Utah - 92
48. Just Wondering - Simi Valley, California - 94
49. Co-Exist - Pueblo, Colorado - 96
50. Tombstones On 167 - Marianna, Florida - 97
51. Room 9 - Victorville, California - 99
52. Looking For Matthew - East Andover, Maine - 100
53. Satan Worshippers - Melbourne, Florida - 101
54. Don't Return - Ozark, Alabama - 104
55. A Tale From Gray Court - Gray Court, SC - 105
56. Bloody Battle Of Indian Rock - Salina, Kansas - 106
57. Who Are Those People? - Smyrna, Tennessee - 107
58. The Yellow House - Lowell, Massachusetts - 109
59. South End Of Newton - Newton, North Carolina - 111
60. Ghost Story of Ft. Riley - Fort Riley, Kansas - 113
61. We Only Stayed Three Days - Ingleside, Texas - 115
62. Pressler Grove - Fort Knox, Kentucky - 117
63. Mysterious Force - Danvers, Massachusetts - 118
64. A House In Warwick - Warwick, Rhode Island - 119
65. Alice - Springfield, Ohio - 121
66. Old Voodoo - New Iberia, Louisiana - 122
67. The Cumberland Area - Cumberland, Maryland - 124
68. The Open House - South Mills, North Carolina - 126
69. The Man in the Window - Newman, California - 128
70. Two Soldiers - Staunton, Virginia - 129
71. Not Friendly - Coarsegold, California - 130
72. Wrecking Ghost - Saint Anthony, Indiana - 132
73. On Downing Street - Greensboro, NC - 133
74. Haunted House on 711 - Powhatan, Virginia - 135
75. Took Us A While - Grayson, Kentucky - 136
76. Spirit At work - Gardena, California - 138
77. Creepy Feeling - Spring, Texas - 139
78. Time To Move - Santa Barbara, California - 141
79. Friendly Soldier - Fort Scott, Kansas - 142

80. Lonely Innocent Soul - Fort Wayne, Indiana - 143
81. The Giggling Sounds - Cannelton, Indiana - 145
82. Our Antique Store - Charleroi, Pennsylvania - 147
83. The Drum - Azusa, California - 149
84. The Pool Table - Norwalk, California - 150
85. A Friendly Old Lady - New Port Richey, FL - 152
86. Blonde Hair In White Dress - Fenton, Michigan - 153
87. Haunted Office - Wakefield, Massachusetts - 154
88. Haunted Fort Campbell - Fort Campbell, KY - 155
89. Evil Boy - Sharon, Pennsylvania - 156
90. On State Route 60 - Zanesville, Ohio - 157
91. The Girl Is Emily - Carson, California - 158
92. Feeling Of Being Watched - Dublin, Georgia - 159
93. Happy Room - Sheppard Afb, Texas - 160
94. Room 5233 - Las Vegas, Nevada - 162
95. On The 4th Floor - Guthrie, Oklahoma - 163
96. Standing Guard - Lorain, Ohio - 164
97. From The Open Closet - Lexington, SC - 165
98. The Industrial Park - North Attleboro, MA - 166
99. Cat's Crying - Vallejo, California - 167
100. Old Convent - Belcourt, North Dakota - 168
101. Haunting Spectacle - Columbus, Indiana - 169
102. Lining Up At An Inn - Lenoir City, Tennessee - 170
103. Not Alone - Austin, Texas - 172
104. A Little Boy By The Pond - Athol, MA - 174
105. Red Brick House - Saint George, Utah - 177
106. In The Apartment - Dekalb, Illinois - 179
107. Unwelcome in Maybee - Maybee, Michigan - 181
108. Still Here - Zanesville, Ohio - 183
109. Grapevine Ghost - Bakersfield, California - 184
110. Warning - Pickens, South Carolina - 185
111. In The Middle Of Nowhere - Ubly, Michigan - 186
112. Jeremy - Oklahoma City, Oklahoma - 187
113. I Don't Believe - Highland, Michigan - 189
114. Still Happening - Buncombe, Illinois - 191
115. She Is In The Closet - Greens Fork, Indiana - 192
116. The Husband - Bolingbrook, Illinois - 194
117. A Mass Murder Location - Fort Valley, GA - 195
118. Their Previous Home - Destrehan, Louisiana - 196
119. He Was In The Basement - Sterling Hghts, MI - 198
120. Little Bones - Plymouth, Ohio - 199

121. Cherry Road - Oswego, Illinois - 202
122. A Child, A Teen ... - Carlsbad, CA - 204

1.
Maybe It's Grandma
Athol, Massachusetts

When I was six years old my grandmother Myrtle had died of double pneumonia. My mother and I had lived with her as she was incapable of taking care of herself anymore. I can't remember the name of the street that this happened, but it's the same street as Silver Lake Cemetery just happens to be towards the end across from a large apartment house and near the river and Main Street. Shortly after my grandmother died (about three days) my mom let me sleep in grandma's room.

Now we never used her closet as it was difficult to open, apparently it was either fitted poorly to the hinges and not square or the paint and humidity caused it to stick. Either way it took too much force to open it, so it wasn't used. About 3am I was awoken out of a deep sleep because the closet door had slammed open on its own. I was terrified and lay there still listening for any sound to betray the intruder in grandma's room. After a couple of minutes no noise occurred. I peaked over my blankets, and the door was indeed open. I could feel someone or something staring down at me from the corner over the bed. I started to yell for my mom, but she was sound asleep and didn't hear me. So after some more minutes passed I gathered enough courage to get out of bed to wake my mother. She closed the door, and I slept in my room after that.

A couple of weeks later I was downstairs with the neighbors while mom gathered grandma's things to get rid of. It was my third night of Kraft macaroni and cheese, my favorite. I ran through the kitchen with the other kids, and the baby sitter turned around to drain the macaroni. As she turned, my head collided with the pan. The boiling contents spilled over my head and caused 2nd and 3rd degree burns.

During the time my skin was melting into my shirt I was out of my body and looking down through the house. I could see everyone running around and me standing there crying, though at that moment I felt no pain. I was floating. I noticed I wasn't alone; slightly to the left front of me someone who resembled my grandmother was there with me. Though I often wonder if she was my grandmother because as she turned to face me as though she knew I noticed her, she didn't look like grandma any more. She was skeletal and frightening. She may have been the one looking at me in her room that night. The moment I became afraid I jumped back into my body, and suddenly felt the pain of my burned flesh being torn off as they were taking my shirt off in a panic because I was melting into it.

Once home after spending months in the hospital, my mother reported that children could see a pretty lady up the corner of grandma's room. These kids never met her when she was alive, but when my mother would take out a photo of my grandma with her five sisters they always picked my grandma as the pretty lady they were seeing in the corner. We stopped using the room. It was empty, and it was always cold in there, and the closet door kept opening on its own. We eventually had to move, actually to the large apartment house across the street. Mom used to hear things about the room after we moved. She heard that the heating system in that room had to be replaced three times because it was always cold. The closet door that once was difficult to open wouldn't stay shut. Children kept reporting seeing a pretty lady dressed in white in the corner over where her bed was.

Our strange happenings didn't stop there. Our new apartment seemed to have spirits as well. When we left to go to appointments we'd come back, and the dishes would be on the counter tops, and all the doors to the cabinets were open. They weren't like that when we left. I could sense a young woman had spent time in the attic and was abused by her husband or boyfriend... I think he killed her.

As the years went on and we moved a few more times, people sometimes would report to my mother that a woman dressed in white would come to them in their sleep. She would stand at the foot of their bed and ask "where was Heidi?" My mother would then take out the photo of grandma with her sisters, and every time they would point to my grandmother. Thankfully, she never found me, though I've had past boyfriends tell me that a couple of times they woke up, and I was still asleep, but there was a white see through cloud floating above me. I know my cat can see something. He looks right at it often enough. I don't see anything, but I can sense something is there.

Maybe it's grandma still looking. I've often wondered what would happen if I went back to her room and said her name, what would happen. She's buried at Silver Lake Cemetery under a big tree; it's pretty there. Her son, my uncle, is buried there with her as well as her husband. David her son, Glenn her husband. Maybe someone could ask them if it's her who haunts me.

Submitted by Heidi, Athol, Massachusetts

. . . .

2.
Playful And Weird
Fresno, California

I don't know if it's the places I live in are haunted or if something is following me, but I have had quite a few experiences. I was living in a house right next to the old Sunny Side Drive-in, and we would experience all sorts of odd things going on. Constantly would hear the sound of kids running through the house, like they were running on hard wood floors (there was carpet at the time.) It was very strange. My bedroom door would open slightly then close. You would hear running; then the bathroom door would open slightly then close. It was never a set time. It would happen both in the day time and at night. I would sit on my bed, and my radio would be on across the room, and suddenly it would start to change channels. It was an old radio, so you had to physically turn the knob. I would sit on the bed and watch the dial go from one side to the other.

I would often have things come up missing only to find them in places that there would be no reason for them to be. My house keys went missing only to find them hanging out of the opening to the attic. My step-father's wallet went missing only to be found under the middle of their mattress. When I was 17 we moved to an apartment across the street from McLane High School, and strange things started happening there as well, but not the same kinds of things. We would have the TV suddenly come on and change the channel to a kid's program. I figured it was just a power surge and wrote it off, until one time it happened, and I happened to say off hand "I really don't feel like watching the Disney channel right now," and it switched back to the program I was watching.

If my mother and I argued, light bulbs would shatter in their holders. After I graduated from HS and moved out of state it kind of died down. However, after the birth of my first child it started back up again. I would put him to bed in his crib with no blanket, and then suddenly he was wrapped in one. Or he'd wake up crying, and I'd get up to put a pacifier in his mouth, and he'd already have one. I never felt like whatever was around me was "evil" or "dark," just weird and playful.

Submitted by Winter, Fresno, California

. . . .

3.
Edward The Blacksmith
Hyde Park, Vermont

When I was around 13, my mom and my toddler-aged little sister and I lived with our two cats and German Shepherd, Chico, in a three-story 1800s converted blacksmith shop in North Hyde Park, Vermont on Ferry Street. My mom and I and our family and friends that visited all had paranormal experiences there. While living there we were restoring the building, and we had a great respect for the house and its property, and nothing that occurred seemed violent or malevolent; it was just unnerving at the time. Through research we came to believe that the presence was Edward, the blacksmith that once owned and worked in the building.

Starting from the bottom, the house had a basement that I never went into, though my mom did. The first floor was a family room, the size of the whole house with the back having a separate laundry and tool room. The second floor had the kitchen, living room, my little sister's room and a bathroom. The third floor was a converted attic with my room and my mom's room at either end and a closet and office between them. There are woodstoves on the first and second floors and huge decorative grates in the floors that allowed you to see all the way through the spaces from my bedroom on the third floor down to the stove on the first floor. It was both awesome and creepy!

Our first incident happened in the middle of the night after our housewarming party. My mom's brother and his girlfriend were getting ready to go to sleep on the futon on the first floor in front of the woodstove. Both of them heard a man call our dog by name, "Chico!" to come down the stairs to where they were. We were all super freaked out by it but tried to ignore it. Chico seemed fine; he ran to the voice with his tail wagging.

More things started happening; I'm not sure about the order. We got home one night, and my sister and I were sleeping in the car while my mom ran to unlock the door and go to the bathroom. She couldn't find her key and was struggling to get the door open and was in a real hurry. Suddenly, the door opened for her. Having had numerous experiences with paranormal activity in her life, my mom took this well, even thanking the ghost for his help!

He wasn't always that friendly though. Another time she was playing jazz on her grand piano on the first floor, and the tool room door loudly slammed behind her. She was startled, but reacted by communicating back to him and saying "Fine! I'll switch to Classical!"

One day my mom left for work before the school bus picked me up. Her boyfriend at the time was still in bed on the third floor, and I was outside waiting for the bus. I looked back toward the house and clearly saw someone staring out the middle first floor window, where the original large sliding blacksmith doors were. I thought it was my mom's boyfriend putting wood in the fire, looking out to check on me. I waved and walked back to the house to say good morning. I opened the door with a smile that quickly fell off when I found there was no one in the room, and the boyfriend was still snoring upstairs.

There was one incident that still has my mom and I questioning ourselves to this day. We were both upstairs in our beds. It was around 9pm, and we were both awake reading before bed. The lights in our rooms were the only ones on in the house. My little sister was at her father's house for the night. Suddenly, the sound of an enormous pane of glass shattering into a million pieces filled the house, and we both bolted out of our beds, running for each other. We raced together down the stairs toward the living room on the second floor. We had both assumed that my mom's giant antique round mirror had fallen off the wall. We turned on the light to find the mirror perfectly safe. We searched the entire

12

house, every window, picture, sliding glass door, untouched and no broken glass anywhere. That was a hard night to fall asleep, but we managed.

We lived there for a few more years while my mom gradually refinished the house and its gardens. The activity lessened and eventually stopped. We joked that Edward had had enough of living with three girls. I moved out, and my mom and sister stayed a few years more. Then when my mom moved in with her now husband, I came back to the house to help clean and prepare it for selling. The house was totally empty of furniture. It was a sunny day, and I had the windows and doors open and music on. I was by myself. My mom was going to join me after work, and I was also expecting a friend to drop by. I had swept, mopped, and oiled the wood floors on the first floor, and I was in my little sister's room on the second floor. The walls were a beautiful dark blush color with fairy decals scattered everywhere. It was my task to carefully scrape them off, and I had my back to the doorway. I can't remember if I heard a door opening, but I do remember the weight and speed of someone running up the stairs to the second floor and walking up to the doorway of the room I was in. I assumed it was my mom or my friend, and I kept scraping as I waited for them to identify themselves. They didn't say anything.

I turned around; there wasn't anyone there. I was alone in the house. I dropped my scraper, ran down the stairs and out the door, and sat on a rock in the sun until my friend got there. My mom showed up shortly after, and I told them both what happened. They both believed me, and we looked around the house together. On the first floor, coming out of the tool room, we clearly saw large bare-footed footprints in a scattered pile of sawdust. Keep in mind that I had just thoroughly cleaned the floors. My mom and my friend had just gotten there; none of us had been in that room, and all three of us had our shoes on the entire time. Not to mention that when we held our feet up to the prints, they were almost twice as big and had an extremely wide gait that was awkward for us to mimic.

That was the last time I was at the house, and I have to say I think Edward was saying goodbye. Either that or maybe he was glad the fairies were finally coming off his walls!

Submitted by Alayna, Hyde Park, Vermont

. . . .

4.
Haunted Building On Ackerman Drive
Lodi, California

This is a very true story of poltergeist activity on Ackerman Drive in Lodi. This is an industrial area with no houses only businesses. Well I am not quite sure of the year when things started to happen where I worked. I would say probably from 2006 on for a few years. It first started with some photos of some equipment I took. There were orbs in the photo. Now most orb photos are dust or moisture in the air that are just retracting the light. Orbs that are just that get far too much credibility as spirit activity. The truth is most orbs are absolutely nothing but what I described.

Now there is this orb that is different and is illuminated and seems to have a mind of its own when caught on video. This type is like a glowing light in a dark room. Well, I was taking still photos on a digital camera, and one of these orbs was a ball of light. Now being a scholar of the paranormal for years I didn't pit a lot of thought into it. I just knew that orb was different from all the other which were indeed moisture and dust. It was a foggy day and very moist outside, and I was taking these photos in a warehouse with most of the dock doors open. I showed it to one of my co-workers, and he thought it was strange, and it was forgotten.

One evening I happened to be working late, and I was alone in the office. Everyone had left, and I was just typing on the computer, and I heard what sounded like a heavy box hitting the floor. It was extremely loud, so loud it extremely startled me. I called out a co-worker's name who had left about a half hour before the noise, thinking he came back and had dropped the box on the floor in the entryway of the office that I am unable to see from where my desk. It was not the employee coming back. This noise came from nowhere. There was also a roll of about ten thick posters that a vendor sent us rolled up and standing straight up. When the noise had occurred these posters fell over. I didn't notice they had until I got up to investigate the noise and saw them lying over. I stood them back up and jumped all around them to see if I could get them to fall over. They wouldn't. Like I said they were thick posters rolled up, and they were sturdy standing up. Now the poster falling was on video. We had a security cam that caught the poster falling over, but nothing else appeared on the video. I wish I had the video today, but I do not. So this loud sound and posters falling over are unexplainable and just one thing that happened that has unknown cause.

A co-worker and I watched a box of heavy steel track flip over right in front of our very eyes. We knew that we had a spirit in the building. I was standing once in the middle of two other employees talking and a wind blew right through me, but this wind was not felt by the other two people standing with me. It was a hot summer, and though I can't say the wind was cold it was cooler than the temperature. It was strange that this wind only went through me. There were a lot of little things that happened like loud noises in the warehouse and thrown paper clips on only my desk. This spirit seemed to direct its attention mostly to me.

Another night I left work, went home, ate dinner and then came back to do some more work. It was dark and raining that night. And I brought my Chow German Shepherd mix dog with me. The dog stared down the entry way all night. It's about 20' hallway that leads to the door which for me is blocked, by a wall but the dog was about 15' straight across from me and could see the door. She was staring and every once a while barking and looking anxious as if she knew something was there. I saw nothing. The window is tinted, and there is a light very similar to a porch light you would at your house, but this made the glass door look from the inside of the office like a mirror because of the type of tint, so you could not see out the door unless you went right up to it and looked out. Well I am doing my work, and the dog is still staring down the entry way. The next think you know there was a loud bang on the

16

door as if someone had hit it with a closed fist but not with the knuckles, with the side of the fist. Anyone who would hit that door with their knuckles to get that loud of a bang would have broken their hand.

Now this scared the hell out of me, and the dog was going nuts barking. I knew I had to investigate this loud bang on the door. Remember just looking down the hallway I couldn't see through the glass door. I just saw a reflection of me, the dog, and the inside of the office. I slowly walked towards the door. I was thinking the whole time when I got to the door which was locked by the way "what in the hell am I going to see?" I got to the glass door, and I put my eyes and my hands on each side of my eyes to get a good look at the outside, and what do I see? Nothing. There was no one there. There was no car or any sign of anyone. I got my keys and leashed the dog, and we went outside to see if anyone was there. Nobody! Unbelievable! How could this occur, and no one there. This building is haunted. I had already known that, but when things don't happen every day you tend forget and then bam, another experience.

There were many things that happened there, like paper clips being thrown on the desk, shadows after hours in the dark warehouse. Some say they saw brief apparitions. I never did. This building on Ackerman Drive in Lodi, California is haunted. I don't want to give out the business or the address. People need to have their own experiences and not be paranoid because of prior experiences. It makes people's imagination run wild. Thanks for reading and every bit of the story is true. I cannot explain it, and I believe it to be paranormal.

Submitted by Anthony, Lodi, California

. . . .

5.
Evil Eyes
Maple Shade, New Jersey

In 2004 we moved in to a town home in what use to be Maplewood now Park Crossing. My wife and daughter seemed content, but I had a very uncomfortable feeling after the first 48 hours in the apartment. I really couldn't put my finger on it, and my wife thought I was crazy. I just kept going on and on about how the place doesn't feel right to me, and I was starting to get annoyed at myself. My aunt insisted it was because I had to get adjusted to a new place. Things started to get weird. We had two touch lamps in our bedroom on both sides of the bed. They began to turn on and off at night. They each had three levels of brightness, and they would take turns going through each level, on and off and sometimes both going at the same time. Eventually, we had to leave them unplugged. We figured it was some kind of electrical interference with the sensors.

One evening while unpacking boxes in our bedroom our daughter, who was four at the time, was on our floor playing. She was flat on her back and tried to sit up. My wife and I watched while she struggled as if someone was holding her down. She had a look on her face like she was trying with all her might to sit up but couldn't. She finally said out loud, "let me go!" She was able to get up and when we asked her what had happened she said a little girl was holding her down, but there was nothing there. Not long after that one day after I had taken a shower I went in our bedroom to get dressed and then back to the bathroom to finish up things. As soon as I went back in I noticed immediately that there was an image of a demon looking thing on our shower liner. It was staring right at me with a creepy smile and a long neck. There were evil eyes and little horn looking things on the head. The image was made up of the water droplets from taking a shower. I grabbed our camera and took a picture of it.

18

The image stayed on the liner all day and was gone by the morning. It never happened again after that. I've heard my name being called a few times while trying to sleep. I have also had dreams of being haunted by something I couldn't see and woke up paralyzed. I couldn't move or speak for a good three minutes or so. Very scary, but this is nothing compared to what I went through while living in Pennsauken!

Submitted by Tom, Maple Shade, New Jersey

. . . .

6.
Frank
Spencer, Massachusetts

It was about 1:00 in the morning when my close friend Frank called me. I was deep asleep, so obviously it took a while to realize that the annoying ringing was my phone. When I finally picked up, the line was just quiet. Since I didn't have a life or a wife or anyone to live with, I just walked out of my apartment and got into my car to check on my friend.

When I got there, Frank's door was unlocked and slightly opened, causing me to worry for his safety. There was no screaming or any sound, so I thought the intruder had already killed him. But, when I walked in, there was nobody to be seen except for Frank sitting in the middle of the hallway floor with his hands behind his back. All the lights were off and the curtains were pulled shut. I asked Frank what he was doing, and he just smiled creepily. He finally stood up, and I stepped back because I was slightly terrified. This was not like Frank at all.

Frank swept his hands away from his back to reveal that he was holding a really big kitchen knife and swung it at my right arm. I was too afraid and confused to move. It started to bleed, and when I finally got my senses back, I ran out the door and drove straight home, leaving Frank there. He didn't follow.

As I was driving away, I took one last look at the house where Frank was. He was somehow sitting on the edge of the balcony on the second floor, and his face was streaked with tears. But not regular tears, they were made of blood. He was still smiling, and then a few seconds later, he fell from the balcony and disappeared into thin air.

I never got another call from Frank again for a while, and when I finally did, a month had passed since the incident. We became close friends again, and he has no recollection of that night at all. Sometimes I think it was just a nightmare, but I still have the scar on my arm where he struck me with his knife.

Submitted by Gerard, Spencer, Massachusetts

. . . .

7.
Little Gnome-Like Creature
Camp Lejeune, North Carolina

I'm a military brat, and the time frame for these occurrences is a little earlier than most of what I've read here. I lived with my family in Courthouse Bay from summer 1969 to summer 1971 in one of the eight officers' houses on the south side of Harvey Street. I won't say which one, so as not to disturb the present residents. The atmosphere of that house was extremely oppressive. I recall never feeling happy there, which was quite different from all the other places I lived. It seems I came down with the flu every six months in that house.

The worst incident happened late in the night or early in the morning in late 1969 or early 1970. The house has three bedrooms and a maid's quarters near the garage. I had a bedroom to myself while my two brothers had the other bedroom, and my parents had the master bedroom. I usually wouldn't sleep in my bedroom as nights there were kind of frightening to an eight or nine-year-old kid, and as my brothers' bedroom had two sets of bunk beds, I'd usually sleep in there with them. On this particular night I had climbed down from the top bunk since it was hot and slept next to my brother in the bottom bunk. I was on the outside facing the center of the room while he was over against the wall.

Sleeping on my stomach, something made me come awake. I lifted my head an inch or two off the pillow to see that something was right next to the bed looking down at me. I quickly lay back down, hoping my acting as though I was still asleep would prevent this thing from attacking me. What I saw didn't look human. I saw a small figure standing there that had on dark pants and a light colored shirt. The thing had a face that was too pointed to be human, and what looked like wrap-around sunglasses on. Remember, this was 69-70, many years before Whitley Strieber's book came out, and at the time all I could think of was that I was

22

seeing some kind of gnome or something. That picture on Strieber's book is the closest thing I've ever seen to what I saw that night or morning. I couldn't see a nose or mouth, as the only light was the moonlight coming through the windows. Nor did I ever hear anything. I lay there in cold sweat wondering what I should do and praying that the thing wouldn't stab me. I saw it for only a scant few seconds before pretending to be still asleep, but I know what I saw. I didn't really want to look at it longer than I did, because I didn't want to see a creepy thing like that actually move. That would've been even MORE terrifying. Finally I got the nerve to jump to the inside of the bed such that my brother would be to the outside of the bed and facing the creature. I pinched the living hell out of him trying to get him to wake up and see this thing. When he did and we both looked out into the room, nothing was there.

I recall even telling my dad at breakfast the next morning that there was a man in the bedroom last night. He believed me, and we went from room to room checking the windows and doors, and all were locked. I saw the same being in the middle of the night in my own bedroom once and quickly put my head under the covers and again pretended to be asleep. Other nights I could hear footsteps on the Oriental rug in that bedroom going back and forth and outside the room. My brothers both had night terrors and would wake up in the middle of the night screaming bloody murder that a man was in the house. One of them even described the man as a little gnome-like figure. Many mornings I'd wake up with a bloody nose.

A couple of more odd incidents in Courthouse Bay: my brother was nearly kidnapped near Marines Road and Middle Street by a Marine in a pink Volkswagen Karmann Ghia, and once in the middle of the night, a woman knocked on the door claiming her car broke down and that her husband had left her and ask if she could use the phone. That may be a normal occurrence in some places, but not at an isolated spot on a military base. Who knows what the source of all this was, but I can tell you I'm not lying.

Submitted by Dee, Camp Lejeune, North Carolina

. . . .

8.
A Girl And Confederate Soldiers
Manchester, Pennsylvania

We found a building in Manchester (a commercial property) that we fell in love with from afar. It was out of our price range. Oddly months later, it was reduced due to foreclosure and a tragic turn of events for the previous owner. We ended up buying the property, and within months had our offices moved in. It sits on a quiet road surrounding by farm fields and is on three acres. I work crazy hours and commute an hour each way. It's quiet, and so I don't mind working late. Upon arrival into the building immediately I felt cold and dampness, and would feel as if someone was behind me most times. It was a clammy feeling. At one point I saw fog on the doors and mirrors and thought I saw something in the mirror move behind me. I was a little scared but intrigued more than anything.

One night I worked very late doing office work and felt very cold and tired. Almost dizzy. The drive home would be an hour, and it was very dark out, so I decided to take a quick nap on the floor before hitting the road. No one was there but me. Immediately I fell asleep and awoke to the entire room being shrouded in fog. I was freezing. I knew immediately this was a sign of spirits. I immediately had a vision of a little girl on a balcony in a white dress. It looked like a grand balcony as if she was in a very rich house, not our commercial building at all! She looked like she was dressed in an outfit you would see centuries ago. I then woke up, and it was still foggy and cold in the room. I ran like a bat out of heck to my car and went home.

Months later a friend of mine was at the building and said he saw a little girl in a white dress out of the corner of his eye run across the upstairs. He said he has seen ghosts before and thought our place was haunted. He said she was only trying to play jokes and scare us out of the building. I did a little research on the property but could find nothing prior to our building being on the property. I do know that it was part of a large farm at one point, and the buildings only a few doors down date back to the 1700s. I invited a metal detecting club who found lots of civil war buttons and old silver coins.

Months later I was working late and went to the side door to open it and get some air. I saw a fog in the yard, and what I thought I saw I couldn't believe. I saw a group of confederate soldiers standing there talking to each other. They saw me but carried on talking. They had old time funny style guns and some type of slings around their uniforms as if they had to carry powder in this to make their own bullets. They had old hats and were dressed in old uniforms. They were pointing across the road and trying to read the map, and I saw across the road what appeared to be a camp with a fire and a guy eating. I ran back inside to get my husband who was actually working late too and told him, and of course he thought I was crazy. I went back to the door, but there was nothing there. I know what I saw, and I wasn't scared, but I wanted to know more. I didn't tell anyone besides my husband what I saw.

I talked to the neighbor who said people always found civil war relics on his property. Months later we had our friend come fix some shingles on an overhang that were coming loose. He said while up on the roof out of the corner of his eye he thought he saw confederate soldiers looking at a map behind him. When he looked down they were gone. He was ironically working on the shingles above the side door I opened. He was the same friend who saw the little girl, and I hadn't told him either story. We both saw the same things. I sat down with my husband, and we told him everything. We stood in the center of our building and talked to the ghosts who haunt it. We told them we aren't going to leave, but we wanted them to stay as long as they need to. We told them we love the property and will take care of it. We also asked them to feel free to tell us anything we need to know. We haven't heard from them since. I always wonder why I saw that little girl.

Submitted by Anonymous Property Owner, Manchester, Pennsylvania

. . . .

9.
That Old Place 20 Years Ago
Lordsburg, New Mexico

This happened about twenty or so years ago. Tears in my eyes writing this down; it still gives me chills.

Going down the highway towards Antelope Wells, right when the road curves back south, there used to be an old farm complex. My pops and I used to roam around abandoned buildings in hope of finding buried gold. Usually all we'd turn up were rattlesnakes and rats. So we saw this old abandoned complex and decided to drive out and took a look around. The place was surrounded by about four mobile trailer homes, which my pops decided to look through. I went inside the house.

Now, I've been in dozens of abandoned homes and have never had the feeling of unease that I felt as soon as I walked in this place. It was like someone had put a blanket over me. I felt alone, muted, and terrified. I wanted to run away, but I didn't want to look like a weakling in front of my dad, so I kept it together. That decision still scares me twenty years later.

I walked in through the kitchen. The refrigerator door was left open; jars of muck were still sitting on the shelves. There were paper and wood strewn about the floor. I moved my way into the living room, where a couch sat blocking the front door. There was a dresser that had been thrown against the picture window with clothes still hanging out. I walked into one of the bedrooms. On the bed was a suitcase. It was half packed, and other clothes were lying on the bed. There was a teddy bear inside the luggage, sitting on top of the rest of the clothes, thrown it at the last second it seemed. I worked my way into the other bedroom. Again, another suitcase, half packed on the bed, but on the floor were hundreds, maybe thousands of checks. They didn't have a name printed on them, no address, just blank checks scattered all over

28

the bedroom floor. There was a mirrored closet on the opposite wall. And on the mirror was a note scrawled in what looked like old shoe polish. It said, "Factory. 1989 FOUND something. DARK"

My dad started calling me and said to get out to the truck NOW. He slammed his door and drove about 70 miles per hour down the dirt drive. I asked him what was the matter, and he just said we needed to leave.

He moved away a few years later. I still ask him what he found in the trailers, and he won't say. He said it was best not to worry about. We drove down there a few years ago to go quail hunting, and he was visibly nervous. We drove past the road leading to the old complex and saw it was torn down.

I don't know what happened there, but it still scares me. I've searched for years online for any other New Mexican that may have seen that place, but it seems like it's just a part of a dream. I wish it were. Sometimes I wake up at night, heart pounding, remembering some unseen evil that we uncovered so many years ago.

Submitted by Patrick, Lordsburg, New Mexico

. . . .

10.
Phillip
West Palm Beach, Florida

I grew up in West Palm Beach, and most of that time my family lived in a duplex in Pheasant Run, a complex on Gun Club Road. During our time in this house my family experienced many paranormal occurrences. Toys would move on their own; we'd hear and see things. There's one main repeated experience that follows us to this day.

When my younger brother was somewhere around six; he started interacting with an "imaginary" friend named Philip. He talked to Philip every day. My sister and I would be alone at home with him, and we would often hear him in his room alone talking to Philip, or we'd hear him banging around. When we'd go in his room to find out what he was doing he'd say stuff like he and Philip were just wrestling. I often thought he was a bit too old for an imaginary friend but never thought much of it.

However, something happened that made me believe Philip was far from imaginary. One day I was upstairs alone brushing my teeth in the bathroom located in the hallway. The door was open, so I could see the hallway from the corner of my eye. Then suddenly I saw a little, chubby, curly haired figure running towards me. My brother used to put a pillow under his shirt and run into me for fun, so I thought it was him doing this. I decided to wait till he was about to bump into me and turn real fast and scare him, but when I did this there was no one there. I searched all the rooms and couldn't find anyone. I went downstairs where my mother was the only other person home and asked where my brother was. She informed me that he was staying at a friend's house. The next day I retold my experience to my sister and brother to which his reply was "oh that was just Philip. "

Philip continued to be a regular part of his life until the day we moved out. Months after we left I asked him if he still saw Philip and he told me Philip had only visited him once since the move. After this we have a few more moves where we relocated in Georgia. The same thing happened; he just gets a few visits from Philip which it seems as though Philip is just checking on him. The last time there was a Philip experience was last year. I was home from college visiting my parents' house. I was sleeping on the couch, and I woke up to the sound of footsteps in the space between my brother's door and the bathroom. The next morning my brother told me he got up in the middle of the night and looked out the glass door into the backyard. He said there standing at the bottom of the steps stood Philip. My brother is now twenty years old. Philip, for some reason, attached himself to my brother. He doesn't know a last name for him, and I've tried to do research but haven't come up with much.

Does anyone know what that land was before becoming Pheasant Run? I have recently come across the name of a little boy named Philip W Thigpen. He was a nine-year-old boy who died in 1928. (My brother said Philip wears white and black clothes that look to be from a past time.) He was killed with his mother and sister in the 1928 hurricane. I know they didn't live there, but I'm drawn to him. I do know his body was taken to a cemetery fifteen minutes away from the residence and buried in a mass grave.

Submitted by Racheal, West Palm Beach, Florida

. . . .

11.
Taking Care Of The Guests
Clifford, Pennsylvania

Years ago my daughter was at camp for the summer in Orson. For visiting day I made a reservation at a Bed & Breakfast in Clifford. It was a lovely place, but I had a strange experience. Visiting day was long, and it was very hot outside. By the time I left I was feeling very ill and had a terrible headache. I headed back to the B&B and was glad nobody was around. The owner had gone to the grocery store, and her husband was way out in the fields cutting the grass. I was eager to get to my room and lie down for a while.

I remember feeling horribly sick; I think it may have been food poisoning because I had eaten some sandwiches that a friend had brought from a deli in NYC, and they weren't keep cold. I felt like I was falling down a well. I was spinning and spinning, and I couldn't wake up. Then someone knocked on my door, but I couldn't move. Hopefully, they would just go away. A while later they knocked again and called my name. I thought it was the innkeeper, but still was too ill to stand up to answer the door. A while later she was very insistent and kept knocking and calling my name. I thought I better at least acknowledge that I heard her and went to the door. She said she was worried and wanted to be sure I was OK. I told her I just had a headache, and I would be fine. She smiled and left.

At breakfast in the morning I mentioned this to the innkeeper and told her what happened. I told her that it must have been the other guest staying there that checked on me but how did she know my name? She told me that guest had checked out the previous morning and that she herself hadn't knocked. Then I told her it was a small woman with dark curly hair probably mid to late 40s with her hair pulled back. Then she said "oh, you saw her too?" Apparently she used to live there. She was so kind I couldn't be afraid of her. I have to say I've never felt that ill before, and I think she may have saved my life. I'd like to go back and see if she's still taking care of the guests that visit.

Submitted by Joanne, Clifford, Pennsylvania

. . . .

12.
Screaming Sheila
Eastland, Texas

It's been forty-three years since my encounter with Screaming Sheila at Ringland Lake. Three of us all boisterous teenagers with attitudes drove out to see this so-called "ghost" and was ready to prove that "she" was nothing but a hoax. We were parked in the dark near the campground laughing and talking about anyone or anything that crossed our minds (looking back I know that we were scared and doing what we could not to show it.) Suddenly the night was pierced with a blood-curdling scream. It was the high pitched scream of a woman, and it came out of the night so suddenly that it raised the hair on back of my neck. I don't mind saying that all the "macho" I came with was suddenly gone.

I was yelling "Get out of here!! Go!! Go!!" It was very apparent that I wasn't the only one scared witless! Both of my friends were yelling, and when we tried to start the car the battery wouldn't crank the motor; it was dead! The screaming continued for what seemed an eternity, and then it ceased as suddenly as it started. We were all yelling and holding door handles (as if Sheila could yank open the locked doors.) Immediately after the screaming stopped we tried to start the car again, and the engine cranked as if there were never a problem. Our exit had to compare to the Indy 500!!

We talked of this night many times, but we never talked about going back. As far as I'm concerned "Screaming Sheila" is the "real deal. " I am now 59 years old, and you still couldn't talk me into going to that lake after dark. My Mom & Dad knew I was scared of the lake, and we were out to eat at K-Bobs when I was in my thirties. They started telling me that they bought some land and asking would I like to go see it? I told them that would be great, but when we left the restaurant it was just after dark, and they were talking as we rode trying to keep me occupied. Then
34

they turned toward Ringland Lake, and I opened my door and jumped out of their moving car! They found out how serious I was that night. As far as I'm concerned, I will never see Ringland Lake again, and if I hear that scream again it will be in my nightmares.

Submitted by Terry, Eastland, Texas

. . . .

13.
Angry Man
Barberton, Ohio

I went for a walk in the walking trail in Rogue's Hollow. I wasn't aware of the legends until after I did some research after my encounter. When I arrived I felt an eerie vibe because not a soul was in site. It was eerily quiet in the walking trail. I had an uneasy feeling about walking in the trails. It was about dusk. I started walking down the trail, and I saw a man in overalls with a hat on standing in the woods. His face was blurry, but I could clearly see his outline. I got very afraid.

I turned around and started walking at a fast pace to my car. The man followed me all the way to my car. I got in the car and was putting on my seatbelt. When I looked up he was glaring at me with an angry look through the window. My hands were shaking so badly that I fumbled trying to start the engine. The man stayed in the same spot looking at me very angry. When I backed the car up he vanished into thin air. I now know why this walking park is empty. I will never venture there again.

Submitted by Gary, Barberton, Ohio

. . . .

14.
Not Welcome
Fort Wayne, Indiana

When I was in my teens, a group of us teenagers would often go to a graveyard located on Cedar Canyon Road, just west of Hwy 327, close to the town of Garrett. On one occasion as we were frolicking and running around among the gravestones, we suddenly all heard a loud scream, followed by the appearance of a figure in a dark monk's robe. The hood was up, but where a face should have been was pitch black. It stood there for several seconds before vanishing before our very eyes. Then we saw a glowing green light moving among the tombstones, but as we got closer to it, it started moving away from us rather quickly. At that point, we all agreed that maybe we were not welcome, so we all got in our cars and left.

I often wondered why we all didn't immediately freak out and run as soon as we started experiencing these strange happenings. I think we were all so shocked and stunned that we kind of just froze in our tracks before gathering up the courage to follow the strange light. Several years later I told a couple of friends the story of what happened that night, and it was then that this newly married couple told me that they were picking up a good friend for a night out on the town. Their friend's home was located next to this same cemetery. I was told the road was Union Chapel Road. As you travel east, it turns into the Cedar Canyons area. My friends told me that as they were waiting in the driveway for their friend, they suddenly saw a dark figure in monk like clothing standing at the edge of the cemetery staring directly at them. This cemetery is still there today. Nothing has changed except maybe some new tenants that have taken up residency behind the old wrought iron gates surrounding it.

Submitted by Mary, Fort Wayne, Indiana

. . . .

15.
Bert And Tilly
Stony Point, New York

I lived on Tomkins Avenue. I know there were spirits in the house. There in my closet were a man, a woman, and their dog (yes, I said dog.) Their names were Bert and Tilly. They talked to me, and my mom thought I was going nuts, but I know I saw them and talked to them. It wasn't till years later these men were looking around our yard. I asked them "can I help you?" They said they were looking around because they used to live there. As far as I knew my grandma and grandpa owned that home long before I was born, so I went in and got my mom. She went out, and I stayed in thinking maybe they just have the wrong house.

About 20 minutes later mom called for me, and I came out. The men were still there. I saw they looked like they saw a ghost. Mom said to me tell these men who lived in your closet when you were younger, so I told them. Then I went on to say how the man was dressed in overalls with a hat. I told them the woman was dressed in a pretty dress with flowers on it. Well, I didn't see colors, but I could see everything like a black and white TV. One of the men started to cry. I asked "what's wrong?" He told me I just described his grandmother and grandfather to a tee. I told them they said their names were Bert and Tilly. Both men just stood there with their mouths opened. I also told them about the little dog they had. I talked to them for an hour about everything. They left so happy and got more than what they thought they were going to get by just looking around.

RIP Bert and Tilly. You were my best friends. They were good people, and some day I hope to see you again.

Submitted by Ginger, Stony Point, New York
. . . .

16.
The Neighbor's Mom
Corona, California

I grew up in Corona off of Border Avenue near the Cleveland National Forest. Growing up my brother, sister, and I all had our own paranormal experiences. The most frequently seen was a shadow man that would stand in my sister's and my doorway for hours. We thought it was our father initially but discovered later it was not. I watched it until the sun came up one day, and it seemed to vanish. This went on for years. Several times while we locked ourselves out of the house, and after about five minutes the front door would unlock on its own. No one would be home. All three of us also saw a little girl around six to eight years old that would look at us then turn and walk away. My brother was ill one night, and he heard a music box and saw her. He thought she was an angel. Around this time I also started sleep walking.

The strangest thing I saw was when I was about eleven years old. I was blow-drying my hair and had my head down. When I flipped my head and hair back I thought I was going crazy. A man in a knight type outfit walked through the wall and disappeared. Someone later told me it could have been a Spanish Conquistador. It was very clear and unexpected. My father still lives in the house. He never really believed us until a friend of my stepmom's started cleaning the house for them. She casually asked who the lady was that visits them. It turns out she was seeing my neighbor's mom who had passed away years ago. Our houses are connected.

Submitted by Tamara, Corona, California

. . . .

17.

The Old Victorian Mansion

Lacon, Illinois

I was looking to purchase a house in Lacon. The old Thompson Keifler house on 5th street was for sale. The old Victorian mansion had been vacated for about five months when we went to visit. The real estate agent got there before us but waited just inside the back door until we got there to go any further. We walked through the large vacant house turning on lights looking into bedrooms and finally got up to the third floor where they had held dances in the past.

After walking around for about twenty minutes we decided we had seen enough and decided it was time to go. The agent shrugged off looking in the basement as it was winter. It was cold, and it was late. As we got back to the first floor and into the kitchen the heat kicked on, and I swear it sounded like people were laughing and in the throngs of a party! We all looked at each other and shrugged. As we pulled out of the driveway we noticed a light had been come back on in one of the attic rooms used as a servant's quarter around the turn of the century. The room overlooked the church across the street, and we had shut all the lights off. We kept going, and so did our agent. It's true the place gave off some weird vibes that after twenty-two years I haven't shaken.... More to come on yet another visit.

Submitted by Jake, Lacon, Illinois

. . . .

18.
Former Resident
Martinez, California

I recently purchased a home built in 1927 on Pine Street. During renovation, random people would stop by to tell me the history of this home. Every single person, including my new neighbors told me the house is haunted. I didn't believe them at first, even though the disclosure letter from the previous owner stated the house was, in fact, haunted.

Before I get too far into this story, I want to tell you there have been no sightings since I asked the ghosts to leave. I appreciate this, since this is my first home, and as we all know, moving is a pain. My first encounter was when I was upstairs working on the house. I heard a very loud crash, as if a stack of plates where dropped in the kitchen. I ran downstairs, but there was no sign of anything - no plates, nothing. I was alone in the house. A week or so after this experience I was upstairs again working on the trim, and I noticed a thin line of water about a foot long, and an inch or so wide, resting on the new dense carpet that was newly installed. I had no water up there; a new roof was just installed, and the water was shut off in the upstairs bathroom.

Shortly after this, while installing the wood trim, I noticed my tape measure disappeared from where I left it, which was right next to the door frame. I went downstairs to grab another one, and when I returned to the upstairs room, there was my original tape measure right where I left it. A few weeks had passed, and I was downstairs taking a break watching TV. I heard a ruckus coming from the upstairs attic, which is directly over the den where the TV is located. It sounded like footsteps and something heavy being dragged across the floor. I grabbed my flashlight and went upstairs to investigate but found nothing. Everything looked undisturbed. At this point I asked the ghost to please leave, that it was my home now in the physical world, and this is my time to reside in the home.

A few months passed, and all was well. My daughter's friend and her three-year-old child needed a place to stay, so I rented one of the upstairs bedrooms to them. About a month later, I was alarmed by the three-year-old screaming in horror and pointing to the top of the staircase. I asked her what was wrong. She frantically stated that there was an "old scary man" at the top of the stairs. She said that he scared her, and she wanted him to leave. I looked but did not see anything. Soon after I kindly but firmly asked him to leave. I haven't had any issues since this, and I'm hoping things stay quiet. On a side note, this home has an inviting warm feeling about it.

Submitted by Doug, Martinez, California

. . . .

19.
Cats Could Tell
Lafayette, Colorado

We just moved in a new place in Lafayette, CO near the King Soopers by Baseline. When I first got the keys I brought a few boxes over to start to put the kitchen in place. I also put a box upstairs in the room. I emptied the box and threw it over the stairs to get it later. Then I went back down to the kitchen. While in the kitchen I heard the same, very loud sound of a box being thrown down the stairs. I was alone though, and not even a pet was here. Hardly anything was here yet. I was startled. I only had one box for the upstairs. I wondered if someone was in the house. I carefully checked. No one, but while upstairs checking again I heard it again.

I decided to leave and dismiss the sounds as house noises that I would soon understand. After two months here I have not been able to find any such source. However, I witnessed the sound at least ten other times since, and others have too. I have not told the children of course, but the sounds have been impossible to identify. I settled on floorboards snapping. It's the best source I can come up with, yet I have checked that, and I honestly now doubt it, especially since the other things started happening. We have three cats, so most of the time I can attribute the sounds to them, but it's when I am alone, and the cats are with me, and I hear repeated found sounds. The sounds are never faint. It is always a loud slam.

The other night, about 1:30 am I was by the fire, my wife asleep in bed. I again heard the sounds in the same room, the other living room. I dismissed it for the sake of the cats. Then one cat came in up to the couch with me, and another. While both of them are on the couch with me I hear it again. I was thinking it was the third cat, though he is old, but then I heard a sound behind me, and it was the third cat eating from the cat bowl in the kitchen. Then he also came up to the couch, so there I was with the three cats, two moved to the floor by my feet. Then we heard the sound again. I say we because the cats looked startled, like dogs do when they are perfectly still, looking at the source of the sound. At least it wasn't just me. I figured the cats wouldn't care, but they did. Then smaller sounds started happening in the room I was in. I decided to ignore them. I was writing a program, and I had to finish testing something. Then, my youngest cat gave that look again, very still and stood up. It was as if she was looking only three feet in front of us. I stopped. I looked all around; everything was silent. Then she shrieked, jumped up two feet straight in the air, and ran to my feet, where the other two cats were. They all looked alert and were looking at the center of the room.

Then my little cat (six months old) got to her feet again, like she was going to run. Then the others. I was done. I grabbed my stuff and went up to the room. The cats followed me, which was unusual, at least the way they did. I told my wife. Yes, I woke her, but I was spooked and needed her to tell me how stupid I was. I am not sure she believes the behavior of the cats, but I am not a ghost person, meaning I don't care or believe in it. However, scientifically we know that there is so much we don't know, and I can't say anything for sure.

One other thing, I have been wanting to ask the previous owners if they had any experiences, and why there was a big cross nailed in the garage. It was so odd. Why did they leave it? Why did they put it there? Why was it painted gold? It was odd. If you saw it you'd know it was too. I removed it three weeks ago. It didn't belong there anyways - why the garage? When we looked at the house there didn't appear to be anything religious about them.

I am posting this because I need feedback. I don't know what I am looking for, but perhaps an explanation for the cats acting this way. Why was she freaked out, like something spooked her that

44

was right in front of us? I have never had experiences before, but I have them every week in this house.

Submitted by Drew, Lafayette, Colorado

. . . .

20.
Black Mass
Bellingham, Washington

I lived in a house in Sudden Valley for about six months when I first came to live in Bellingham. Sudden Valley has its own mystique with so many huge trees and houses built to be a part of the woods. Some houses, like the one I was renting, are built over cliffs on stilts. Because of the way the house was built, (it was built in the mid-1970s according to Whatcom County land parcel info on the internet). I often tried to ignore the creaks and moans of the house as the weather changed or the wood stove heated up the house. However, the first few weeks of living in the house told me that there was something other than the house creaking in a normal fashion.

I started hearing a breathy type voice in the master bedroom, and only in the master. I searched and searched for a reason for this sound. While I'm a believer in spirits and other paranormal occurrences, I am also very logical and believe that many things considered as evidence of a haunting can easily be explained by natural/normal phenomena. As much as I tried, I was never able to pinpoint the noise. What's more, the breathy voice sometimes would be right in my ear, and other times it would seem to be coming from across the bedroom. The noise would occur at any time of the day or night, but it would only be in the master bedroom. In addition to normal creaking and the weird breathy voice in the bedroom, there were also clearly footsteps that would pace the main hallway of the house. After even a few weeks, it was quite easy to tell the difference between the footsteps and the house doing its normal creaking/settling business.

Finally, one night, my husband heard the breathy voice. It's not like he didn't believe me before, but now he KNEW exactly what it sounded like, and he agreed with my "spirit" assessment. Both of us continued to hear this voice on and off, until one day I was sick of hearing it. I told the entity that I could hear it but couldn't understand it and if they would please stop, that would be great. Neither one of us heard the breathy voice for several weeks after that. Then, all of a sudden the noise came back with a vengeance, as now it was a daily occurrence and multiple times per day, not just a few times per week as was happening before. At this point my step-son also started to report that when he closed his eyes in his room, he could "see" a shadow moving across his eyes, like someone was walking back and forth in front of him. (He slept with the lights on at this house, and I have no reason to disbelieve him. Also, we never mentioned the ghost or spirit word when he was around. I didn't want him to freak out!)

One night, after the breathy voice came back, I went to use the en-suite bathroom, and this black mass came up from the floor and blocked my path to the toilet. The mass blacked out the window that was behind it and also the toilet and wall. I could not see through it. I happened to be feeling very ill that night and told the mass to go away as I was sick. For some reason, I wasn't scared at all when I saw the mass, even though I was fairly certain it was the entity in my house trying to show itself to me. After the night I dismissed the mass, I didn't hear the breathy voice again until the week before we moved out of the house. I never saw another black mass either. I couldn't find any information about the house, but I'm certain there was something else there other than me and my family.

Submitted by Heather, Bellingham, Washington

. . . .

21.
No Longer Scared
Warsaw, Indiana

The paranormal experiences I've had started at my previous residence in Warsaw, Indiana from the time I moved in (June 30th, 2008) to the time I moved out at the end of November 2013. I have numerous witnesses and accounts of activity during that time. The following are some of the experiences.

When I first moved in, right away there was a feeling of constantly being watched. At the time I would get off work around 3am. Each night when I would get home I would walk into the house, and it was like I was interrupting an ongoing conversation between two people, with no radio or TV on in the house. This happened several nights.

The basement was where I always felt like there was a more heavy and angry energy. One day I was going downstairs to check on laundry. I was home alone, and as soon as I started down the stairs, I felt two hands on my back and a very hard push. I fell but was able to catch myself and ended up pulling a muscle in my arm. Another time going upstairs from the basement my ankle was grabbed, and I felt the hand and had to shake it lose.

I was told when I purchased the home that the previous owners that built the house had both died in the home of old age, which really didn't bother me much at the time. I had a get-together shortly after I moved in, and one of my friends that is a sensitive came. He did tell me that I had the spirits of an old lady and a very angry old man in the house.

Every experience I or my friends have had has all been so random. The house had an old doorbell that you could hear all through the house. I was told when I moved in that it didn't work, so I didn't think much if it until it started chiming by itself mostly

48

at night. It got so frequent I finally cut the wires to it, and it still continued to chime!

There was an instance where I was in the shower while home alone. The shower curtain opened like someone pulled it back almost a foot. The attic door would sometimes open on its own. One night while I was watching TV and the door to the attic flew open with force like someone wanted it to be open. My dogs ran and barked at the attic stairs for almost forty-five minutes.

There was another time when my boyfriend and I were watching TV, and in the hallway closet a heavy air pump to our air mattress flew off the shelf. Of course after all the things happening my dogs went crazy. My dogs also started fighting each other, after years of being together with no problems.

In the spring of 2011 I had a friend staying with me. One night she was home alone and watching TV. In the home you are able to see the kitchen from the living room, and as she sat there, she was able to see the cabinet door by the stove open. Then a pot came out and hovered about four feet off the ground, and then it was gently set on the floor! Another friend was spending the night after a Superbowl party and got up in the middle of the night to get a bottle for her baby. While she was in the kitchen she heard a door open, and when it opened it sounded like it brushed against the carpet. The weird thing is none of the doors touched the top of the carpet, at least not when I lived there.

In October of 2012 the same friend had another experience during her birthday party at my house. It was an outside party, and she was inside using the bathroom. The house was empty, and when she was in the bathroom she heard what sounded like a conversation between two people through the wall. She even thought there were people in the house, so she called out and got no response.

I would get in the habit of taking just random pictures with my cell phone when I would start feeling like I wasn't alone. I never saw anything with my eyes, but there are definitely things in the pictures. When my boyfriend moved in with me in 2013 we had his kids every other weekend, so we had a room for them. A couple of times we would hear his youngest in his room talking to someone. When we would ask him who he was talking to, he would say nobody. My boyfriend's two children shared a room, and in one corner of the room we would always find dead flies. We tried everything to get rid of them, but we lived in the country and figured we would have to deal with it.

There were times when we did have the kids, and we would be sleeping, and my boyfriend would wake up convinced there was someone in the house. He would grab the gun and search the house. He would find no one. This happened several times. At night we always shut and locked our bedroom door. One night we both woke up to the sound of the door coming unlocked, and we both watched the door open!

There have been instances where I've seen shadow people. Once I was pulling into my driveway, and there was a shadow person standing in my front window. A couple of nights later I was sleeping and rolled over, and there was a shadow person standing in my closet. I would also see shadow people walk across the hallway into each bedroom.

After moving out my parents took over the maintenance of the house until we could get it sold. One time my parents were working in the basement, and there was always a fly swatter at the top of the stairs hanging on a nail. While they were working in the basement, the fly swatter came flying down the stairs toward them. Many times while my Dad was there working alone, and every time he has heard voices. Once he had the door coming into the house from the garage open while he was in the basement. He heard it and thought someone was there, but there was no one but him.

Since leaving the house there are times I miss it, but I'm mostly glad to be out of there. I no longer have to be scared something will harm me or my family.

Submitted by Jennifer, Warsaw, Indiana

. . . .

22.
Creepy Face
Lake Arrowhead, California

I've lived in Lake Arrowhead for 17 years. My small A-frame cabin from the 1920s has few neighbors around; most are vacation homes. You might say my house is off by itself where I lived with my two dogs.

One night I had been in my kitchen making dinner. When you enter the kitchen it's long and narrow with a window above the sink at the end. The kitchen window had a half cafe curtain on it. One dog was inside, the other out on the porch about 20 feet from my kitchen window, where no one could get from outside without going through the fenced yard and passing the dog, a large German Shepherd.

After I finished making dinner, I took it upstairs to eat at my computer when the indoor dog started growling then barking wildly at something in the kitchen. He's part pit and Akita and doesn't scare easily, but whatever he saw got the fur up on his back and made him pee the floor.

I went downstairs and said "WHAT? What?" I walked into the kitchen to show him nothing was there. I had my back to the window and called him over. He wouldn't step foot in that kitchen; he just growled and snarled. I bribed him with a piece of food, but now he was barking and growling at me! I instantly thought something is in here. (This area is known for odd things happening.)

I ran upstairs and got my camera then back to the kitchen. He continued barking at the kitchen the whole time. I snapped about 9 pictures from the living room. Nothing showed up in any of them but one, and I am posting the close up of it.

The shape of a transparent creepy man's face looking in over the top of the curtain appeared in the picture. My heart froze. How could anyone get into the fenced yard and that close to the house with the dog outside unaware of them? Answer... No one could.

The outside dog stood calm on the porch outside wondering what was going on inside. My dog eventually stopped barking and calmed down. Then moments later came in the kitchen like nothing had happened. That is not the first creepy thing that happened in that area.... But the first I caught on film.

Submitted by Maggie, Lake Arrowhead, California

. . . .

23.
Devil's Tree
Port Saint Lucie, Florida

Everybody has heard of the infamous Devil's Tree here in PSL, where two girls were sadistically murdered by an insane police officer in the 60s. He hanged them from the tree and left them there for days. The foundation of his house still remains in the thicket of branches behind the tree. Most of you have heard stories about people being chased out of the woods, and that you can hear the girls scream at times. I always called bull on those allegations because I had been there so many times night and day without experiencing anything.

That changed one night, though, when me and a few friends had just exited the trail onto the canal line. (If you've ever been to the Devil's Tree you'd know the tree isn't far off from the end of the trail.) We had spent a few minutes gathered by the tree; there were four or five of us. As we walked out of the woods, coming directly from where the tree was, we just spent ten minutes fooling around. Only probably a hundred feet or less away was a blood curdling scream. It lasted up to five or six seconds. We all looked at each other in shock, and walked hurriedly back through the parking lot to the car.

We couldn't come to a conclusion. We were all dumbfounded. None of us have brought it up since that night. This happened in, I think, either 2011 or 2012. I will never forget it, and I hate going back to the tree at night, but I've been dragged along a few more times without incident.

Submitted by TB , Port Saint Lucie, Florida
. . . .

24.
At The High Desert Center
Victorville, California

When I was a teenager, I became a performer at the High Desert Center for the Arts in downtown Victorville. At the time, I had no idea that it was haunted, but over the course of four or five years, things happened that just couldn't be explained.

I was about fifteen when we started rehearsing for our first show. Everything was fine except for that awful smell in the restroom. At first, my friend and I thought that maybe someone had a stomach virus and kept taking bowel movements in there every evening, but one Saturday we were the first ones to arrive and the restroom still smelled that way. We asked one of the male performers if he smelled it in the men's restroom, and he said yes, but it wasn't strong. None of us could tune our voices in those bathrooms though. Looking back, it smelled like death or decay.

One night, my mom was late picking me up. I went to the front of the building and sat outside on the front steps. Everyone else but one or two people had left through the back exit. When a creepy guy pulled up and started hitting on me, I quickly went back inside and sat on a couch in the foyer. I could see orbs in the little gallery to the left and a few in the ticket box to the right, but the gallery was the creepiest. The entire doorway suddenly lit up and a figure started to appear. I got up and ran back outside just as my mom pulled up.

All throughout the building, we felt random cold spots, even in the summer. Still, the first variety show went off without a hitch. With the second show (a patriotic revue) my best friend and I decided to go to the same gallery where I had seen the orbs. My friend is an amateur artist, and she was admiring the sculptures and paintings when a door in the back of the gallery started shaking like crazy. The door was blocked off and could only be reached through a hallway that was usually locked. We both ran out, and I went to the hallway door. It was unlocked, but no one was there. The door had just stopped shaking a few seconds before, so if someone had been back there, I would have at least caught them leaving.

We did a diva show the next year, I believe. Rehearsals were fine except for one of the sound guys feeling like there was someone else in the booth with him when he was alone. Then another performer and I made a mistake. The show director came backstage before our second showing and started telling us about the building history. Apparently she had also experienced strange phenomenon. She told us that the building was once a performance hall where service men went to see shows on their way through town. One of the performers had committed suicide backstage. There were stories about him haunting the backstage area directly behind the stage. Then the director said that there was a one-eyed man who haunted the sound booth. Another performer and I started making jokes. She joked about the backstage ghost, and I joked about the ghost in the sound booth. We stupidly made fun of them.

That night everyone's performances went smoothly until it came to the other performer's set, the one I had been joking with. She got out there with her acoustic guitar, hooked the guitar to the amp, and started playing. Toward the end of her second song, someone started messing with the amp backstage. It would go up extremely high then turn down very low. At the end of her last song, the amp fell over on its own.

We were creeped out, but I was next, and I had to go on. Like the previous performer, my first song was just fine. Toward the beginning of the second song, my backing track turned all the way down. I looked up at the sound guy, who looked confused and started messing with the switchboards frantically. We finally got it back on track ,and I finished my set.

After the show was done, the sound guy informed me that the volume button had never moved, and he could not figure out why the music had been muted. I think we had upset the ghosts so badly that they wanted to mess up our performances and knock us down a peg. I haven't been back since. My ex, my mom, and my now-deceased grandmother each told me that they had had their own supernatural experiences in that building.

Submitted by Kimberly, Victorville, California

. . . .

25.
Ghost Cop
Richardson, Texas

This happened to me in 1987 when I was twenty years old, coming home late after a night of working as a waitress at the Fast & Cool Club. It was late, probably close to 4am, because we were open late for dancing, even after last call, and I always had to stay and clean up the place. Plus, it took me a while to get home. I was driving north on Central expressway. I took the Spring Valley exit going west toward Garland. The highway was pretty empty, as was the street, once I exited. There was a Red Lobster restaurant at that exit. Anyway, there was no traffic, and I was pretty much alone. I took the exit and then turned right on Spring Valley. I immediately saw a police car in my rearview mirror, so I pulled into the Red Lobster parking lot, which was lit with street lights but empty. I knew I hadn't been speeding. I had no idea why I was being pulled over.

The police officer was working alone. He was tall and slender medium build with dark hair. He wore a uniform and had a thin gold plate bar name tag on his left breast pocket that I distinctly remember, although I wish I had paid actual attention to the name itself (I have no idea what it said.) He told me I had been speeding, which I couldn't have, since I slowed down for the exit and drove slowly to turn the corner onto Spring Valley. He hadn't been behind me on Central. I would have seen him; I'm sure of it. My window was rolled down for him. He asked me for my license, and I handed it to him. He took it back to the squad car with him. The squad car lights were still on flashing. I waited for several minutes, wondering what the heck he was doing back there. Then I looked down and saw that I was holding my driver's license. I was flabbergasted. The cop car was nowhere to be seen. I was so freaked out that I actually drove all the way around the Red Lobster parking lot looking for that cop. The clock showed that no time had passed, other than the couple of minutes I had sat there waiting. Ghost cop?

Submitted by Susan, Richardson, Texas

. . . .

26.
Not Happy
Martinsburg, West Virginia

We lived near the police station off of exit 16 Edwin Miller Blvd. I was told an elderly gentleman committed suicide in the area that our houses were built. Our first experience was when we heard thumps coming from upstairs when my children were sleeping. Thinking he fell out of bed, my husband and I went running upstairs to check on him, but he was sound asleep. My grandma used to watch the computer come on late at night. She would hear the front door open and close, and then hear footsteps going upstairs. We used to hear the garage door open and close. My husband and kids would see a black shadow man. My grandma and cousin saw an older man: one in the woods, the other in the dining room.

I had a friend stay overnight in our spare room. She left in the middle of the night. The same night my Grandma said the door flew open by itself, and it was bolted shut. My children saw the microwave oven door open and close by itself in the basement. You would run through the hallway because you always felt like someone was watching you. My son said he saw a black shadow with red eyes. During that same time I heard footsteps above me in his room. After that we sold the house. As far as I know, no new activities have been reported. Last time we drove by the house, my oldest son saw it outside on the stoop over top the steps. One week after we moved trees fell down across our neighbor's yard, all the way across our yard, taking out the kids' playset. The week after that our basketball net disappeared. I don't think the ghost was happy when we moved.

Submitted by DCW, Martinsburg, West Virginia
. . . .

27.
He Liked Women
Tempe, Arizona

We looked at a house to rent, and as I stepped into the house, a strong smell of roses came over me. Later I asked if anyone else had smelled it, and no they didn't. After moving into the house we found it was infested with scorpions. On the walls, ceiling, floors they were everywhere. We had pest control out every week to spray. The numbers finally went down to almost nothing. Then all of a sudden they were back. My husband had a dark figure with a hat standing over him when he was awoken at night. He had strange dreams about it.

My visiting grandson and son were attacked after going to bed, and the bedroom door shut and would not open. The lights would not come on, and my grandson was pulled forcibly under the bed by an unseen force. My son yelled, and finally the door opened. We moved. Others have moved into the house since and the men always seem to leave. I found that this house liked women, tolerated men, and hated kids. Then after being tired of picking up a neighbor's garbage they throw over the fence into the alley, I started taking pictures to make a complaint and got this spirit in the picture. We also found a dead bird in the kitchen fan over the stove. We don't know who it is. However, we understand a man who originally bought this house when it was built committed suicide in the house in the 60s or 70s. The house is off Mill Avenue on Grandview. My husband now believes in ghosts.

Submitted by J, Tempe, Arizona
. . . .

28.
She Ran Fast
Irvine, California

The weirdest thing just happened. I don't know if I'm just tripping out, but it made me seriously scared. It's about 1:30AM right now, and just about 30 minutes ago I was walking my dogs in my apartment complex. Down at the end of the street I saw a young woman dressed in a short sleeveless black dress. Now that I think of it, it's kind of chilly outside... What was she doing dressed like that?

Anyway, my eyes aren't that great, so I couldn't make out her face or anything, but it looked like she was staring right at me. She stood with her shoulders square, directly in my direction. As I minded my business and picked up after my dogs, I saw her turn to the side once. Then she turned back, looking at me again. I didn't think much of it, so I continued down the street toward her. I lost sight of her as I walked behind a tree, but when I look back in that direction I saw her RUN away. She ran FAST! It almost looked like she was gliding down the street. It wasn't like a blur, but I clearly saw her gliding down the street. It didn't look like the normal body motion of a person running. If I were to describe it, the way she ran was like large dog or coyote running full speed.

The freakiest part is that there was absolutely NO SOUND. It was dead silent. I could hear birds, but not one footstep from her. She was close enough where I know I should have heard something. She was probably like 20-30 yards away from me when I saw her run. I really don't want to call it a ghost just yet. I'm tempted to go out there again, but to tell you the truth, it freaked me out. I think I will take a look one more time though.

Submitted by Rob, Irvine, California
. . . .

29.
Hawaiian Warrior
Honokaa, Hawaii

I live in the Pa'auhau community, which is called the "Land of Sunshine. " It's a beautiful place, but has a history behind it. It was here that King Kamehameha the Great nearly lost a battle. The battle of Pa'auhau was told to be very gruesome with many deaths. There is a small horse pasture owned by a friend of mine above Ho'lauae Street (referred to as 'First Street') and a large cattle pasture above that. I live on First Street, and you can ask anyone who lives here as well that on many nights, there are strange noises that come from the pastures. The cattle seem to be spooked by something, you can hear them stampeding around and making this god-awful sound that resembles a dying person or something. The two resident horses will often let out a shrill neigh, their hooves thundering on the dirt.

One night the noise was too much, and something made me walk outside onto the street to see what the horses were fussing about. My first guess was that a stray pig had wandered into the pasture, but as I stepped out into the street, I saw something. The moon illuminated the street, and I could clearly see this tall muscular figure standing there... Almost confused. He had on traditional Hawaiian warrior attire, with a very long spear grasped in his large hands. He was looking around him. I remember seeing his head darting from left to right as if he had stumbled into a new world. Finally, his eyes fell upon me. His eyebrows furrowed, and he took a hesitant step towards me. He was about ten feet away, but I still had to tilt my head upwards to look in his eyes. After a few moments, he turned his back towards me and walked down the street. I then followed him. He walked up this small slope leading up to the horse pasture's fence and knelt down beside something. Then suddenly he vanished.

The next morning I went out to that very spot, and there it was. I have noticed it before, a large circular rock that leans against the fence. If you were to drive down First Street on your right, you will see the same large rock where the Hawaiian warrior had vanished.

Submitted by Kahea, Honokaa, Hawaii

. . . .

30.
Outside The Door
Canyon, Texas

I used to live at a house on the corner of Turtle Dove Lane and Rockwell Road. My family and I lived there for close to five years, till 2012. My dad had moved up to Amarillo, and my mom in Canyon. I stayed at the house for a few months to keep it clean and tidy for any showings that may come there. I was 20, so having a house to myself was pretty cool. My first night alone, however, I was going to sleep, and had the master bedroom doors closed which was where I was.

I was watching a movie on my laptop with my headphones on (these are the kind that cancel out the noise pretty well.) About half way through the movie, I could hear a group of people that were talking right outside the doors. I could not make out anything they were saying, but I felt as if I was being watched because every time I paused the video to see if I could try and understand them, they would grow silent. When the video started again, they would talk. I eventually mustered up the courage to open the door and see if anyone was there, and there wasn't. The freaky thing about it was on that particular night, I heard it without the headphones on. As I walked to the door, it grew louder. I put my ear against the door before I opened it and again could hear the group talking, but could not understand what was being said.

Outside the door when it was opened, there was nothing. It was cold, however. This happened a few times. Then one night as I was trying to go to sleep I had something else happen. I was almost asleep, kind of in between being awake and being asleep, when in the ceiling above the bed, I started hearing footsteps. It sounded like someone was wearing big heavy boots. They would start at one end of the bedroom, walk across the room to the other side, (crossing over my bed) and then stop and cross again the other direction. This went on for at least an hour, and it was late at night. To say I was paralyzed with fear would be a mild statement. I called my girlfriend at the time and asked her to stay on the phone with me throughout the night. I checked the attic the next morning and found nothing. The way the roof slopes over the bedroom on that side of the house, it would be impossible for someone to be pacing back and forth. This happened several more times, and was so loud it would wake me up at night.

Eventually I told my sister what had happened while she was over visiting. While I told her, it started up again. I was both glad and scared at the same time. Glad that she heard it and knew I wasn't crazy, but scared because I didn't know what it was. We both got out of there. Later after I moved out of the house, my dad and I went over there to check the place to make sure it didn't need to be mowed, etc. On the way I told him about the things I heard. I will never forget he looked at me in astonishment and said "I didn't want to tell you this, because I knew you were over there alone". At times I would wake up at night and hear people talking outside my window, but every time I looked there would be no one there. At one point I was so scared I grabbed my pistol and went out and investigated and found nothing.

Submitted by Nathan, Canyon, Texas

. . . .

31.
Ghost Dog of Esters Road
Irving, Texas

Growing up in Irving, Texas back in the 1970s, I heard of several ghost stories that involved the area near Esters Road where my family lived. The story was that a man was killed and still haunted a square radius of 183 to Northgate and 114 to Esters Road. I heard reports indicated that he would appear only after the sighting of a large German Shepherd who acted as though it wanted you to follow. If you did so, the dog would lead you to a bush or a clump of trees then seemingly disappear with no visible signs of leaving it from every direction.

At age eleven or twelve I was skeptical or unafraid until one day when I went for an afternoon ride with my pony. I came upon a German Shepherd standing in the middle of the pathway. I hesitated to go forward. Then the dog turned and sauntered toward a bend in the road to the right a couple of feet away. It then turned abruptly into a bush on the left, but I did not see it come out of the bush. Concerned and a little curious that it was the Ghost Dog of Esters Road, I reined my pony around the bush several times finding tracks leading into the bush but not out of it. Of course there was no sign that the dog was inside the bush hiding. After my curiosity was satisfied I continued on my afternoon ride excited that I saw something that only a few have ever seen.

Submitted by Patty, Irving, Texas

. . . .

32.
An Elderly Lady
Sayre, Pennsylvania

Once upon a time I lived on E. Packer Avenue in Sayre with my mother and little brother. There were some weird sounds, orbs, and even cold spots, but as a skeptic I tried turning them into ghost stories for my friends but honestly telling myself there was another explanation. That is not the point of this story however.

The house next door is the one I know is haunted. When I was about 15 I had just got out of the shower and opened the curtains in my living room to see the street lined with police cars from Sayre, Athens, Waverly, PA State Troopers as well as south Waverly which had a police department at the time. This was before the fancy Dodge Chargers. All together maybe there were around 10 or so police cars. No ambulances or fire trucks yet, so as a paranoid teenager in east side I ran out the back door through the neighbor's yard to a friend's house in Waverly and didn't stop till I got there.

About three days later my mom told us that the lady next door was yelling at her daughter, and the grandmother stepped in and got pushed down the stairs and died. The house sat vacant and looked horrible for about five years. The typical haunted house you would picture, but at this time no stories. Then at the same time of the flood in 2011 a family from Williamsport moved in, and we helped them a little bit here and there with things like floors, walls, windows, etc. Just being neighborly.

They never got the house totally finished. It still kind of looks pretty bad, but it has come a long way, and I had lived at this house several times with them. Once after they went back to Williamsport, I always felt uneasy in that house like something was watching me. I felt cold spots, but we blamed on the draft.

We also heard footsteps and whispers. I didn't believe in ghosts at the time; however, I was always interested in ghost stories.

Then one night I don't remember where my girlfriend and son were, but I was lying in my bed late at night. All lights were off, and I had not yet fallen asleep. Then I saw her. It was not a full apparition or an orb but kind of like a white cloud. The room got cold. I felt like someone was in the room with me, and this cloud entered the room through a shut door. It slowly went down in front of my dresser then up in front of the TV and round the corner or the foot of my bed to my son's play pen. The Pooh, Eeyore, and Tigger started to sway back and forth. Then the window started to shake as if it was storming outside, but it wasn't. I lived in that part of town for many years and knew it wasn't headlights from a car or anything else. It was the first time I had seen a ghost. After that I had seen her flash by my face in the living room while playing Xbox and in the kitchen while getting a drink.

Every time I feel the cold chills and the feeling that you're not alone. You can tell the difference between these white flashes and another form of light. Then a few years later I think my friend said they saw an apparition of an elderly woman in a dress with no real emotion on her face. She came down the stairs, looked at them, walked towards the kitchen, and vanished in the middle of the room. The weird thing is I had not told them the story of the old lady or even that I believed it was haunted.

I have this belief that of all the people who have died on this earth over its history that probably nine out of ten locations will have some sort of ghostly activity. I fully believe now, and it just seems to make sense to me. I hope it shows you that this type of stuff is actually pretty common.

Submitted by AJ, Sayre, Pennsylvania

. . . .

33.
There's More to Life
Sugarloaf, California

I remember visiting in Moonridge, California in 1968 and stayed overnight in a house my girlfriend's family had just purchased. While asleep upstairs with a cat on my bed, I saw the cat jump off the bed, and nudge the door open as it ran out. I looked up to where the only window in the room was and saw a dark shadow of a shrouded person standing, staring out, blocking some of the moonlight. Then it turned, walked toward the bed, stood over me, placed one hand on a bible on the chest of drawers next to me, and then proceeded to reach his other hand into my brain! The electricity I felt as this happened in my head was something I will never forget. I was speechless and afraid to move. Then the ghost turned, walked back to the window, and continued to look out of the window. I watched for about twenty more minutes, and I didn't want to frighten the parents or my girlfriend, so I kept it to myself until the following morning, when we met for breakfast.

A few months later they moved. I was in the service, and I never heard if they had any stories of their own to tell. I can only think this was a ghost of a person caring for a sick or old person who may have died there previously. At least I hope that is what it was. I could not see any face features, but it was semi-dark, even though it was a bright lightly cloudy full moon night. The shrouded figure was about six feet tall. The family had never had an experience before, or they refused to speak about it. It was funny how the conversation was very short about such an eerie happening. I thought that was odd at the time too. I had seen a dis-embodied hand while driving through the area on another night. When I asked the girl next to me what she thought she saw, and she saw exactly what I thought I saw, even though I didn't tell her what I had seen first. How it could have traveled from the driver' side to the passenger window and out was scary since I was driving at about 35 miles an hour. Nowhere else have I ever had

70

an experience like either one of these, although I had used a Ouija board when I was a child and guessed the date and time my cousin would have a baby months later. There's more to life than what we can often explain!

Submitted by Jack, Sugarloaf, California

. . . .

34.
Third Floor
Mackinac Island, Michigan

My husband and I stayed at the Island House Hotel in 2010 when I was several months pregnant with our second child. I had read that a few months prior to our visit a ghost hunting association had visited the hotel and gathered quite a bit of evidence from the third and fourth floors. We stayed in a room on the third floor.

The first night I had a very uneasy feeling in the room. I stayed awake most the night, but I didn't see or hear anything unusual. The second night, probably so exhausted from not sleeping the night before I was finally dozing up around 3 am when I felt the entire bed shake. It was as if someone had grabbed the end of the mattress and shook it as hard as they could. I immediately jumped up and looked over at my husband, who hadn't moved and was snoring. I knew I wasn't going to fall back to sleep, so I sat awake, and no more than five minutes later the fire alarm went out in the hallway just outside our room. The entire hotel was evacuated for nearly an hour, and we overheard the fire department ask the front desk staff when they arrived, "third floor again?"

I lost a pair of shoes here as well. I had them right by the door to wear when we checked out. When I went back to the area to gather everything to go they were gone. I called the front desk within an hour after leaving, and they said they couldn't locate them anywhere. We checked into a bed and breakfast for the next night, and our innkeeper asked where we had stayed. Upon telling him unprovoked, he told a story about staying there years ago and being woken in the middle of the night to his bed being shaken. At that point, my husband was a believer too!

Submitted by Aubrey, Mackinac Island, Michigan
. . . .

35.
Comes With Cigar Smell
Natick, Massachusetts

I moved to Natick in 1969; I was ten years old. We moved into a house on Washington Ave. When we moved in the house hadn't been updated in years. The living and dining rooms had huge gray cornesses over the window, and the attic and basement were full of the previous owner' stuff. I was down the Cape with my Grandparents when my Mom, Dad, and sister moved in. My first night in the house was early September 1969. That night I kept hearing a man's voice say "Jeff. " It sounded like it was coming through the heating vent and was metallic sounding. I heard that voice every few days until my Mom and Dad moved out in 1995.

There were many shadows, especially in the basement near washer and dryer. A lot of times plates would move by themselves; pictures would fall off the wall. My Mom was pushed down the basement stairs once. I flew off the top step upstairs and hit the wall before falling five feet to the landing. My sister was doing a Ouija board in her room with friends and was told by the board she would die young. She was twenty-three when she passed from complications to Friedrich's Ataxia, a rare muscle disorder. I could go on forever. A lot of times you could smell cigars when things started happening. No one in my family smoked cigars.

Submitted by Jeff, Natick, Massachusetts

. . . .

36.
Check On My Baby
Tickfaw, Louisiana

Many odd stories have been told about the old Lallie Kemp Hospital on Highway 51 between Tickfaw and Independence. It used to be a full service hospital in the state-run Charity Hospital system, but was turned into an outpatient clinic a number of years ago, and most of the old wards were closed. Human figures and moving lights have been seen through the windows inside the closed wards at night in recent years.

My personal experience was from 1986, when I was a physician in residency training at the facility. One night about 10:00 pm I was walking from the apartment where the residents stayed, which was in a separate building, to the main hospital. A woman was standing near the path crying as I walked by. I asked if she needed help, and she asked if I could check on her baby. I asked her name, and she didn't reply. I went into the building and told the night nurse to get security to help her, thinking she was very upset and possibly psychotic.

The nurse looked at me oddly and walked out the back door to look. She came back in and said "there's no one out there. " She then told me that multiple people had reported a woman walking the halls of the maternity ward who would ask about her baby and then disappear. I went back out, but did not see the woman. At the time, this was way out in the country, and it was quite unusual to see a person at night, particularly outdoors, other than the handful of night employees, who I knew on sight. No one seemed to know who she could have been, but there had been a number of recorded deaths of both mothers and babies at the hospital. Could this have been a ghost of one of them? I don't know.

Submitted by Jeff, Tickfaw, Louisiana

. . . .

37.
Standing In The Basement
Anderson, Indiana

I lived on West 7th Street by the old park. I lived there with my dad until I was nineteen. My sister used to always tell me about how there was a guy and his mother that lived there before we did. She'd tell me that the guy killed himself in our basement and that not long after that the woman had a heart attack and died in the house. (This was later told to me by my father as well. He stated that they got such a good deal on the house because it was supposedly haunted.) Well when my sister was three she'd tell my mom about a woman that would come out of her closet at night and play with her. It obviously freaked my parents out enough that we had a lock on our closet door. They also had a religious aunt come over and perform a pseudo-exorcism of the house.

My parents stated seeing weird things around the house too such as what looked like a cloud or puff of smoke moving through the house. Anyways, when I was fourteen I was getting ready for school. I went to the basement to get clothes out of the dryer. I grabbed my clothes and headed back up the stairs just to realize I'd left the light on. I turned around to flip off the light and saw a man standing in the doorway. I could see right through him, but I could still see him standing there. It looked like he was peeking around the corner to watch me walk back up the stairs. I freaked out, ran back up the stairs, locked the basement door, and began yelling for my sister. She was as freaked out as I was. I haven't been in that house in a few years now. It currently sits abandoned since my father has passed away.

Submitted by Nikki, Anderson, Indiana
. . . .

38.
The Lewis Gratz House
Yoncalla, Oregon

My name is Tracy. My family moved into the Lewis Gratz house when I was about four years old in 1968. This house was a large four-bedroom, two-story structure with a balcony and sizable attic. It was absolutely beautiful with full of crown moldings and decorative fixtures (hinges doorknobs with skeleton keys) with an indoor well that was covered by flooring in the enclosed back porch. The first night there, after supper we settled down to watch TV and were interrupted by the sudden blaring of the radio in the kitchen turning on by itself. My dad being a military man would not even allow us to say the word ghost, much less, listen to what we were experiencing. We had items going missing or broken, faucets turning on by itself, and the ghost of a man that would visit my oldest and younger brothers, events that would get us into trouble. We dealt with this just fine.

A year later dad left mom, and she went to work at the Why Not up the street. Then activity got worse. On a regular basis, a big black cloudy looking thing would chase us out of the house, laughing. This was frightening, and I would stay gone until I knew I would eventually have to come home. My older brother and sisters had friends to board with (one sister stayed a lot at the Applegate House.) My younger brother went to the babysitter when I got to my room upstairs (the one with the balcony.) I would close the door, shut the light out, and cover my head. I would then hear heavy but somewhat quiet, as if trying to sneak footsteps come up the stairs. I used to count the steps walk into my room, then creep down the hall to the other bedroom. Sometimes it would stand at my bedside a good bit before leaving. In the morning, I would wake up and see my doll lying in the floor twisted up in a way not natural to one just tumbling out of bed (hair ratted up arms and head turned around and so forth.)

However, the bible I slept with was never touched. I never looked to see what paid me these nightly visits. I knew it wasn't a family member, and I just knew better not to. It may have been the man ghost that my brothers saw when we first moved in. They slept in that room where it used to go at night. I also saw a woman ghost. She wore a plain light gray dress, looking out of the upstairs window, but I only saw her once. One of my sisters used to see a ghost she described as an Indian wearing white fur and anglers on its head that would appear in a bedroom left of the front room and move into a closet under the stair.

Well, this was a very scary house, and we dealt with this for five years. I wish I knew the history of this house, but my efforts have failed. I just live too far away to dig up any information and would welcome any. I will certainly appreciate it. Thank you for taking the time to read my submission. I'm sorry I have no photos, just my story...

Submitted by Tracy, Yoncalla, Oregon

. . . .

39.
In Belfaire Trace Subdivision
Dacula, Georgia

I live in Belfaire Trace Subdivision in Dacula, GA. My husband
and I have lived in this neighborhood for fifteen years. We have
had paranormal experiences in our home from the very beginning.
I was afraid at first, but over the years I have just learned to live
with it. The first thing that started happening was I would see dark
shadows upon waking, as if it was hovering beside the bed. When
I would try to focus on it, it would disappear. My husband tried to
convince me it was the shadow of our bathroom door beside our
bed. I wanted to believe that. The last thing I wanted was for our
house to be haunted. However, it doesn't matter which way I'm
facing, whether it's toward the bathroom door or the opposite
direction, I still see them.

Sometimes months will go by, and nothing will happen. Then I
may see them two or three nights in a row. At first I wouldn't stay
in the house by myself overnight when my husband would go out
of town. Whatever it is, it doesn't seem to be dangerous, so I do
stay here alone occasionally. I do feel uneasy when I have to.
Another paranormal experience that occurred in our home
happened around seven years ago. It was quite unbelievable, and
we have never discussed it with anyone, besides each other. We
were both in our master bedroom in the bed, and we had turned all
the lights off to go to sleep. I was still awake with my eyes open,
just thinking about different things when this ball of white light
came through the wall in our sitting room. It moved around
erratically in our trey ceiling above the bed. Then it exited back
through the sitting room and literally disappeared through the
outside wall.

I have since learned that the proper name for this ball of light is an
orb, but at the time I had no idea what it was. My husband hadn't
experienced anything up until this point. I was glad that he was

there to see it. He had not seen any of the black shadows. I felt better that he had been a witness to this experience with me. We were not the only ones either. My cat at the foot of the bed saw it. She jumped up and was starring at it as it moved along the ceiling. Most of the activity seems to occur upstairs. We have had doors slam upstairs when we were both downstairs, and there was no one else there. This happens more often than I like to admit. It's not just a door closing either. It is a major slam. My husband's first thought on this was, perhaps, it has something to do with the return vent that is in the hall upstairs. We do not keep any windows open, because I have asthma. Since there are not any windows open causing any type of suction. I don't see how the return plays a role in this. There is so much pressure behind the slams. I couldn't close a door that hard if I tried.

We had another experience a few years ago in our guest room that my husband uses as a TV room. My husband came home from work, and when he went into his TV room he turned around and yelled downstairs "What were you looking for in my TV room today?" I said "I haven't been in your TV room today. " He seemed angry, and he acted like he didn't believe me. He asked me the same question again, and I gave him the same answer. I was starting to get mad myself because I could tell he still seemed not to believe me. That was when he told me that all the doors to his movie cabinet were open. I said "well, I have not been in there. You must have left them open. " He told me he did not, and we got into an argument about it. His TV room is one of the hot spots in the house for paranormal activity. The door to that room slams more than any other room.

I will close with this final experience. I don't know if you can call it an experience or not, but I think that it is. I was in the master bathroom upstairs cleaning out from under our bathroom sink when I heard my husband coming up the staircase. He had been doing yard work outside. He was out of breath from climbing the stairs at a fast pace. He said "What do you want?" I said "What are you talking about?" He said" you were calling me. " I said "no I wasn't. " This has happened five or six times since this first episode. My husband will think he hears me calling his name, when I am not. I don't know if anyone else in the area has experienced any paranormal activity. We don't talk about it with neighbors or anyone really. I guess it would take something horrific happening for us to leave. Nothing aggressive has happened toward us, and I hope it never does.

Submitted by Bella, Dacula, Georgia

. . . .

40.
An Imprint On My Soul
Lakewood, California

I have had several things happen to me in Lakewood. I used to live on Monogram Street and was driving at night to the nearby Wal-Mart. I had stopped at a 4-way stop and started thru the intersection when I saw a kitten to my left on the grass outside a corner house, chasing (I guess) a moth, so I kept watching it till I was just about across from it when it darted into the street after the moth and in front of, and I thought under my car. I screeched to a stop and pulled over. I resigned to the feeling that I had to have hit it, but when I looked into the street, there was nothing there. I looked on the other side of my car, in the yards of both houses and found nothing. I even went back the next day and knocked on the door to the house, whose grass I had seen the kitten at and asked if they had a kitten, that I may have possibly hit it the night before. They looked at me like I was nuts.

I had my young son with me, and he saw it too. I have had pounding on my bedroom door where I lived, and 3 people who lived in the house from one family died... At least 1 in the house. I also would give my son a 2-way radio to be able to reach him when he went out to play, and he to reach me. One day he went to a park by our house and library, and while he was there playing with some kids, a bully started beating up on him. At that same moment I heard him call me over the radio. I answered him, and he said he was on his way home. I told him to be careful and told him I loved him. He said bye or okay, and the radio went dead. When he got home he told me about the bully, and I asked why he didn't tell me when he called on the radio. He said "mom, I didn't call you on the radio. "

My son's room was right off the kitchen which was one of the dead family members, and he would tell me that he saw a lady in a hat carrying a tray in the kitchen. She would peek in and check on him, or pat his head, so he wanted his door shut with his cat in the room. Then he would say he saw shadows of people in the kitchen under his door, but when he called out nobody answered, and he knew we were not in that room. We did glass beads in the detached garage of the house, and we had a security camera faced towards the sliding door back entrance to the house. On several occasions we saw a little boy sitting and playing with two of our cats by the trash can.

Also when we had not yet moved into this house we were driving to the freeway to go home. We were driving east on Del Amo, just east of Studebaker (I think.) We were in the slow lane about 3 am and looked out the driver's window to a coyote running alongside my car. He wasn't spooked; he kept looking over at me, and I was talking to him. I turned to my boyfriend and son to see if they saw it, but they were sleeping. When I turned back he was gone. There was no sign of him in the rear view mirror. All these things have left an imprint on my psyche/soul.

Submitted by Anonymous, Lakewood, California

. . . .

41.
Buzz's House
Mill Valley, California

My aunt Ruth and her husband bought their house off the Shoreline HYW on Ross Drive in Mill Valley, CA. Back in 1951 they lived there for many years. There was a big Portuguese cemetery up on the hill. You could see a big tomb stone from way down in the valley in the back yard if you looked up there. As a kid I didn't like to look up there and see it. My uncle Buzz let the bushes and small trees grow high behind the house by the fence to block it from view. He said to me I don't like looking up there either at that big grave stone.

That was in 1968. He later died alone in the house of a heart attack while Ruth was gone visiting her mother in Milw. Ruth felt so guilty that she wasn't there to maybe help her husband when he had his fatal attack. He was found dead on the living room floor next to the couch. That was in 1977. He was buried up in that very cemetery that overlooks house from high above on the hill.

I went up there hiking up the hill in 1988. When I got in there I didn't see the big stone I can see from the bottom. I wasn't sure where it would have been. There were empty crypts and other weird stuff. It started to get later, and the sun was going down fast. I felt it was definitely time to get out of there. Later as I was staying there in Buzz's old bedroom a wind blew down the hill, and the blinds rattled like a buzzing sound. I've stayed there many times before and never heard that before ever! I said to Ruth who is since passed on too, "Buzz said he didn't like that grave yard. " She said "oh, in later years he said he did and would like to be buried up there to watch over the house and me. "

She sold the house in the late 90s and moved back to Wisconsin to be by her family as she had cancer, and most all her friends had already died. She sold the house. She later died in 2000 in Milw.

WI. The house I notice has sold many times in short spurts. I thought "why has this place sold some times at quite a loss?" It's a prime area for commuters to San Francisco. Many celebs live in the area, Tom Smothers, Grace Slick, Jerry Garcia of the grateful dead all lived in the area. I wondered if Buzz maybe didn't like the strangers in their house.

Submitted by Brian, Mill Valley, California

. . . .

42.
Sue
Collins, Missouri

My daughter named my parent's ghost Sue because the name could be a girl or a boy according to Johnny Cash. One night at mom & dad's last week I got out of bed and used the bathroom between the guest room and the master. When I was done I walked down the hall and was right inside my room when I heard someone run across the hall into the bathroom (as if they were in a hurry and had been waiting for me to finish.) They turned on the sink faucet only for a couple of seconds and then turned it off. I turned to look down the hall, and I said my daughter's name because I was annoyed she made noise running loudly and then didn't have the light on or the bathroom door shut.

I thought maybe she was sleep-walking. I turned on my bedroom light, so I could see down the hall. I saw my husband wincing in bed due to the light being on. THEN I could see both of my kids sleeping on their designated sofas in the living room. This stopped me in my tracks! Someone was in the bathroom and mom & dad's door was shut, so I knew it wasn't them.

I walked to the bathroom and turned on the light. No one was in there. I stood in the hall way frozen and re-enacted every move and noise in my head. It wasn't a coincidence to creaking floors or plumbing issues. I knew what I heard. I went back to bed and slept looking at my door while trying to figure it out but soon fell asleep (luckily). I told the story to my family the next day. That's when my daughter named her.

That next night we were all talking and telling stories. The front porch light had been on but suddenly went off and then back on. We all screamed 'Sue!' It happened a few minutes later again. We then turned off the light switch and said "there may be a short. " The next night the light was on but never flickered.

That night I was sleeping. My back was to the door. My covers were only over my legs, and my shirt was raised up exposing my back while I slept. I was awoken by a cold small hand on my back which brushed downward. I thought it was my son as he'll sometimes come to me in the middle of the night. I rolled over to see him, and I started to say 'Hi BUBBY,' but no one was there. At that moment I realized it was Sue and that Sue must be a small child.

In all of this I never felt threatened or in danger. It must be Casper the friendly ghost. Nothing else out of the ordinary happened, but I have to say the basement leaves me uneasy.

Submitted by K.D., Collins, Missouri

. . . .

43.
Mystery Woman
Spokane, Washington

My boyfriend and I recently moved into a house near the VA hospital that was built in 1954. Although I was very persistent in asking if anyone died in the house, I was told that realtors in Washington have to tell me if there was a death in the house, and there was none. My boyfriend has seen several sightings of a young woman with long wavy hair wearing a white nightgown in the basement. She will open the basement door and walk down it. She would be walking right up to him and just stand there.

I have asked two neighbors that have lived next door for many years and knew the previous owners and their children. They both said no one has died in the house. My boyfriend also has accused me several times of talking on the phone in the middle of the night or hearing me talking to someone, but all the times I have been asleep. I am usually very perceptive to ghosts, and I have not felt or seen this "woman" or heard voices in the house. I would really like to know if anyone can tell me how to look for information into finding out about this ghost since we are both new to Washington. I can't help to wonder if living next to a cemetery has anything to do with it.

Submitted by Laura, Spokane, Washington

. . . .

44.
Wolf Pen Gap
Mena, Arkansas

I am not someone that believes in ghosts or paranormal as a general rule. This was a time I questioned my own beliefs. One night I was hunting out in Wolf Pen Gap just leaning up against a tree on a hot day. It started getting dark, and it seemed I was going to go home empty handed, so I decided to pack up and head home. When I got up I smelled this foul odor that was like an animal that had been rotting for a while. It was so bad that I nearly gagged. I looked around and about forty yards away across a field on a rock was a creature.

This thing had long black hair all over it and seemed to be floating about a foot off the ground. There were no legs at all. Then it just looked at me and stretched out these arms out front and came at me quiet fast. I felt this sense of dread was over me. I pulled up my gun and yelled "stop, or I'll shoot." It just stopped, put its arms down, and began circling me as I walked back to my truck. When I got in and started the truck it was only about six feet away. I drove off and looked up one more time to see if it was there, but it was gone. I will never go hunting out there again. I won't even step near Wolf Pen Gap ever because of what I saw. I still can't explain what it was.

Submitted by Brian, Mena, Arkansas

. . . .

45.
Energy Perimeters.
Westchester, Illinois

This whole neighborhood is haunted. My grandma moved to North Roosevelt Road, and from day one they have been seeing shadows walk across upstairs and standing in the doorways at night. We would always hear the wooden closet doors rolling open when nobody would be up there. One time my mom was there alone and was walking to the kitchen, and something banged so loud above her head; plaster almost fell on her. Once when I was little I was sleeping with her upstairs, and something was scratching her foot. It woke her up, and she thought it was me. When she rolled over I was sleeping. That knocked out right there in her face. I grew up and ended up buying the house next door. Big mistake! The same thing happens here.

Sometimes I could hear someone run half way down the stairs and stop. When I look nobody will be there. One thing that used to happen was strange but not very scary. I would hear guys talking in the house. It was hard to hear and pin point where it was coming from; it was like in the walls. I assumed it was residual energy coming from the basement because it sounded like guys sitting around playing poker or something, as if they were smoking and talking. Then I was talking to my neighbors and found they ALL had similar scary stuff happen like hearing babies cry, water turning on, and lights going on and off.

Recently a couple moved in, and when I met the wife the first thing out of her mouth was asking if I knew of her house being haunted. She said her normally lazy dogs were going crazy barking at walls and what-not. Well I did some investigating and figured out why. The land is on the same latitude of old cemeteries to the west (Queen of Heaven and Mt. Carmel) and the East (Forest Home). Forest Home Cemetery was originally a Potawatomi Indian burial ground. The Des Plaines River runs through it. These Indians buried their dead along the water. Now my block is also parallel to the Des Plaines River and Addison Creek, so it could be a kind of energy perimeters. I stopped being scared when a house full saw "me" walk into my room carrying my baby, but they were so scary when I walked in the back door. I was outside the whole time, so they saw an apparition of us, but we're alive and well. Strange but true...

Submitted by Jmoney, Westchester, Illinois

. . . .

46.
A Cowboy In The Hallway
Mission, Texas

Close to MHS. When I was younger about eleven or twelve years old I lived with my great grandma. She has lived in that house for many years, and one of her sons that used to live there passed away. When a family member would come over a strong scent of cigar would hit them. They all knew it was "Louie," my grandmother' son. There was also the smell of fresh roses, which is a perfume my grandma (my mother's mom) used to wear, said her husband. My mother never got to meet her because she passed away giving birth to her.

As I was living there, I'd get these pains in my stomach at 2 or 3 in the morning, and I'd wake my grandmother up with me. She did everything she could to take the pain away, we'd sit in the sala till I'd feel better, but I started to realize she would be very tired in the day, so the next time I got the pain I got up and went by myself to the sala and sat. I was scared because I always felt something, so I turned on the TV. The hallway light was on. I put my head down in pain, and in the corner of my eye I thought I saw my grandma.

As I picked up my head, I looked into the hallway, and I saw a shadow. It looked like a man dressed like a cowboy. As he was walking down the hallway to the end, he turned around and stared at me. I was in shock. I felt my body frozen, and when he turned around the feeling went away. I screamed as I ran to my grandmother's room and woke her. She laid me down and said "it's ok. Everything's ok," and I feel asleep. I told her what happened in the morning, and she couldn't believe it. All she said was "it was a bad dream. " I still clearly have the picture in my head till this day.

Submitted by Anonymous, Mission, Texas

47.
Jeffie's Still Here
Provo, Utah

In the mid 70s a BYU freshman hanged himself in Budge Hall. I lived on the same floor a few years later and a lot of really freaky stuff happened. Nobody really wanted to talk about it, but apparently the student was named Jeff or "Jeffie" and got bullied a lot by other students. His roommate came back from Christmas break, opened the door and found Jeffie dead, suspended from the ceiling. He left a really bad, angry note.

For as long as I was there, the Budge 2100 floor never had a Resident Assistant that lasted a whole semester. They always quit. My first RA confided to me that he had terrible nightmares where Jeffie would visit and tell him "secrets. " He wouldn't tell me what the secrets were. He eventually had to go to the hospital because he couldn't sleep, so he quit, but he showed me Jeffie's picture from one of the BYU annuals, written on the back of it were the words "I'm still here. "

I had a good freshman year. I mean, we were all a little freaked out about the story, but it only really seemed to bother the RA's. I did notice though that rooms would sometimes get really cold for no reason on an otherwise warm day. The only time I really freaked out was a night when I woke up and had to use the bathroom. I walked down the hall, did my business, and was about to wash my hands when I swear I saw a flicker of movement in the mirror behind me. My skin began crawling. The hair on the back of my neck stood straight up, and I was frozen with illogical horror. I sat for what felt like an eternity, unable to move, with a terrible, indescribable feeling of darkness in my heart. When I could move again I ran all the way back to my room. I'm not ashamed to say that forever after that I peed out the window.

I don't know if Jeffie is "still there," but he certainly made freshman year interesting for us. I've never been back to the Budge 2100 floor, and I never really want to.

Submitted by James, Provo, Utah

. . . .

48.
Just Wondering
Simi Valley, California

My Story is one that involves all five of my family members. My folks bought a brand new home in 1964 on Appleton Road near Fitzgerald. My brother was four, and my sister was three (I was born in 1966.) My brother told me when they were moving in he and my sister were playing hide and seek while my parents were unpacking. My brother ran into my sister's room and opened the sliding door to her closet quite quickly thinking she would be in there. Instead, he saw a very serious and angry looking lady glaring down at him. He nervously waved and said "hello," but she just continued to look down at him. He tore down the hallway at brakeneck speed to the garage were my parents were.

This was the beginning of a series of events that occurred for the entire time we lived in the house (which was fifteen years.) One of the events that I most remember was when I felt like something was sitting on me. Another was when I felt something breathing in my ear VERY closely. One of the last big things I remember was hearing what I thought was my mom getting comfortable on the bunk bed below me. (Dad would snore loudly.) Something told me it wasn't "mom," and I turned my light on and flung my head down really fast only to find... Nothing! The bed was still made and untouched. I heard ALL the sounds of someone in the bed getting comfortable, and there was no one!!!

I would also hear what seemed to be conversations between a man and woman, very faint, without one word being discernable. Also, there were lots of footsteps up and down the hall. There are too many happenings to list here, but these events were experienced by all family members in one way or another.

I would LOVE nothing more than to know why the land is not right. We had fairly close neighbor friends that had paranormal

94

events as well. I REALLY wonder if current inhabitants have experienced anything.

Submitted by David H., Simi Valley, California

. . . .

49.
Co-Exist
Pueblo, Colorado

I live in a house near the fairgrounds that has had a few paranormal things happen. The first was shortly after we moved in. We had these Christmas figures set up in front of the television. As my wife and daughter were watching, the snowman figure did a complete 360 in front of them. The second was my grandson. He was playing a video game when a friend took a picture. In the first picture the image of what looked like an old woman appeared on the screen, and the next image she was standing right next to him.

One time late at night as I was preparing for bed, I went to the bathroom, and a young girl's voice asked "is the dog in here"? I looked to my daughter's bedroom, and she was fast asleep. Why it asked that I can only think, it may have been a day that we let the dog in the house as he rarely came being a large outdoor dog.

One time a family friend who had no prior knowledge of any strange happenings here slept over, and the next morning proceeded to tell us our house was haunted. She saw the image of a young girl walking in the house. One time my cell phone came up missing. I looked for two days, and then all of the sudden it turned up on a couch that I had been using for two days.

A person once ran out of gas in front of our house. When the lady came to the door to use a phone she told my wife that a friend's husband committed suicide in the house. I got angry because you just don't tell people things like that about their house. Might spook someone bad. We have come to grips with the activity here but don't feel it is malicious or evil, so we just co-exist with whatever entities are here.

Submitted by Ronm, Pueblo, Colorado

50.
Tombstones On 167
Marianna, Florida

I think it must have been around 2004 I left Marianna on my way to work at Bay Medical Center in Panama City. I have been taking HWY 167 for years both day and night with no problems. I always worked the night shift. It was either October or November I can't remember which, but I do remember it was getting dark early. I was on Kynesville Road, and I slowed down enough to make a left turn on to 167. Just as I already made the turn and began to speed up to go on, then suddenly on the left corner there were three old looking tombstones.

The one in the middle sort of stuck out front a little bit. In front of that one was the ghost of a man, only he had no legs. Apparently he had been killed on that road many years ago and had been cut into half. He was simply hanging there in front of the stone. He was dressed in early 1900s style. He was wearing a long sleeve red shirt and a black vest as if he were all dressed up for a special occasion. He had black hair which was combed back in the middle with a receding hair line on each side. His eyes were a deep chocolate, and we made eye to eye contact.

I kept going up the road in shock as I knew that those graves had never been there before. It must have been about 4:30 in the afternoon as it was just starting to get dark, and the upper atmosphere was darker than the ground. Normally there are three white posts of some sort on this corner with the middle one protruding out just a little, but that evening they had been converted to tombstones. That broke me up from driving that road at night, and instead I go all the way down Kynesville Road and left on 231. I know it takes 15 to 20 minutes to get down 167 as I have timed it to make sure I have enough time to get off before dark sets in. However, the very next year I got careless. I was off that night, so I slept at home in Panama City. I got up a little later than I should have, and I started to my mama's house in Marianna. I was in a hurry, so I would not have to go the long way.

When I reached HWY 167 it was about to get dark, but I thought I could make it before it did. I turned onto 167 and had barely made it past the bar a little way when all of a sudden I saw him again. This time he was down inside the ditch with his back to me, and he was floating down the ditch going the same direction as me, but I passed him. I do not go that way at night any more. Some time later I was on the road during the day, and just before I got to the Marianna end of 167 where the white pipes are I saw a wreck. A very nice pickup truck had gone over a fence, and the back was suspended in the air. The police were already there, and it was a single vehicle accident. I kept going, but till this day I wonder if the driver saw the ghost and had a wreck. I have tried to research and find out who the ghost is but have had no luck. Apparently three people were killed at the same time.

Submitted by Reba, Marianna, Florida

. . . .

51.
Room 9
Victorville, California

I worked at an old nursing home in Victorville in the maintenance department, fixing things that broke and keeping the facility operational. It was rumored Room 9 was haunted. It remained unused most of the time I worked there. It was always colder than any other room in the hospital. Even in blazing hot desert summers it was chilly. It was said that Room 9 was a makeshift morgue back in the day before local services were available, as they waited for county coroner's to come pick up the deceased. There was a story I heard of a terminally ill patient once housed in Room 9 who would stare into an empty corner frozen with fear at something nobody else saw.

Another long term resident asked to be moved from the room because every night, a figure would stand next to her bed, and she couldn't sleep. I was doing some repair work in the bathroom of Room 9 one day, (it wasn't in use) and I was the only person there. I shut the room door to get some peace and quiet while working, and in the mirror over the sink I saw someone walk behind me while I was in the bathroom doorway. I stopped what I was doing and turned around to see who was there, but I was alone. The direction it went was toward an exterior wall. There was only one door to the room, and it was the opposite direction it was traveling. It would have had to disappear into a solid block wall.

A medical staffer who worked overnight shifts would tell me of talking and laughing emanating from Room 9 as he made his rounds during the wee hours. Again, it happened all while the room wasn't occupied. I don't work there anymore, but I'm sure the oddities in that room continue.

Submitted by Dirge, Victorville, California

52.
Looking For Matthew
East Andover, Maine

East Andover is a friendly little town just like most towns in Maine, but when the sun sets it's a different story. This story starts out with a couple of teenagers sneaking out in the summer of 2013. The two teens were walking down Farmers Hill. They snuck out for a late night swim at the covered bridge which was about two and half miles away. The night was crisp, and the teens were feeling the adrenalin that came with it. About half way to the beach, there was no cell service, and both of their phones started vibrating. Not thinking much of it, they turned them off and continued walking. One of the teens stopping in her tracks; the other one turned around and asked what was wrong. The teen remained speechless but managed to hold up her finger and point straight ahead. The other teen turned around and froze.

A woman who seemed to be mildly glowing was walking towards them. She had long blonde hair and had a white dress on. She got within 20 feet of the teens then stopped. The teens still didn't make a move. After a few heart stopping seconds, the woman took another step forward and appeared to be crying. She started to speak, but it was in a low whisper. She said that she was lost and couldn't find her little brother, Matthew. The teens were still motionless and in shock. The woman turned towards the woods and walked. When she got to the tree line, she vanished.

The teens decided to go swimming on a different night. They turned around a walked back to where they were staying. They haven't really told anybody the story. But how would I know? You see, the teen that could only manage to point, was me. I've been in some paranormal situations before. But this, was by far my favorite. I hope that the woman found her brother.

Submitted by Shhh, East Andover, Maine

53.
Satan Worshippers
Melbourne, Florida

Many years ago I lived in a home near F.I.T. The home had been unoccupied for about two years before my ex and I moved in. This house had the worst insect roach infestation that I have ever seen. It took many treatments to eliminate them. As time went on, we started noticing odd things such as noises, our car keys and other things not being where we put them, and feelings of a presence, etc.

One night we decided to sleep on the fold-out couch in the living room due to back problems. Late in the night we were awoken to crashing sounds and glass breaking. As I tried to jump up, my ex shoved me back down on the mattress and told me that someone was out on the enclosed porch which was about fifteen feet away on the other side of the sliding glass door. The porch was enclosed with walls, an outside door, and two windows and could be accessed from the house by the sliding doors. I could only hear the noise. It sounded like the enclosed porch was coming apart. Almost like a tornado had hit it. We had four cats at the time that stayed out in that room at night. I could hear them hissing and screeching as if in fear.

My ex would not let me get up and told me NOT to move. We lay still for a very long time being very quiet. The noise stopped after a few minutes, but my ex insisted that we not move. He was scared to death! Finally he quietly got up and turned on the lights. There was no damage to the porch area. However, each of our four cats was backed into a corner hissing and growling. They had peed all over the floor in that room. I have never seen cats act like that before or act so afraid. We could not even get near any of them as they hissed and tried to scratch us.

My ex went to the kitchen sink, pour some water in a cup, did some kind of Catholic Blessing with the water, and started sprinkling around the porch. He was very frightened by whatever he saw, but would not talk about it right away. He finally did confess to me that he saw a figure standing in the middle of the room. He said it was large and looked like it was wearing a cloak or something. It just stood there. My ex saw the debris flying around the room as well as the cats. All these things were hitting the sliding glass door. However, when he turned on the lights, there was no damage at all. Just the frightened cats. He was very upset, and his recall of what he saw scared the daylights out of me!

I told one of the neighbors about what happened, and she told us that about a year earlier a van full of people moved into the vacant house. She thought they were renting the place, but there were never any lights on, and these people were really weird. Finally, one day they strung up a wild hog in the front yard and slit it open to drain the blood and freaked all the neighborhood children who ran home and told their parents. Parents called the police who came out to investigate and found these people were not renters but squatters and ordered them to leave, which they did.

The house was on the market cheap as a fixer-upper when we moved in. While trying to clean the place up, we found under a pile of trash on the enclosed porch and a 5-point star inside a pentagon shape. At first we thought it had been painted on the floor, but realized it had been burned right onto the middle of the concrete floor. Neither of us knew what it might have been at the time. We only later discovered that a pentagon star is a symbol used in Satan worshiping -- one more creepy thing about this house. We now wonder if those squatters were indeed worshiping evil. My ex saw the tall figure in the middle of the floor that night. The cats didn't calm down for almost 24 hours. One of the cats walked right to the middle of the floor, sniffed the floor, hissed, and backed up. We knew then that something was really wrong with this house.

Other things continued to happen in the house, but nothing quite as alarming as that night. My mother did not like the feeling she got when visiting us. She was a woman with a strong Christian faith. She kept telling me that I needed to move out. She sensed something wrong with the house and would rarely visit and never stayed very long. Eventually, we moved. The house has gone through several owners since. I don't know if others living there have had any problems with this house, but it has been nicely remodeled, and the back porch is now a part of the interior house.

I have heard that sometimes you can get rid of a problem in a house if you remodel the area that seems to be generating the issues. I hope that all this remodeling has indeed cleared the house of whatever was going on there. To this day I would never want to live there again, and I think I've only driven by there only once in all these years. I still got an uneasy feeling about the place. There are things we do not truly understand, and I think this house was one of those things for me personally!

Submitted by BC, Melbourne, Florida

. . . .

54.
Don't Return
Ozark, Alabama

In Ozark, Alabama there was an old white house on a dirt road near my home. Every night when I walked my dog I always heard the sound of children laughing from the house. My wife never believed me until that one night I brought her along to investigate. We arrived at the abandoned home at about 11:30 pm. We sat in my Ford pickup truck for about ten minutes. I left her in the truck while I walked around the property. I found an open window, so I climbed inside. It was dark, but when I turned on my flashlight I saw an old wooden room filled with seeds. In the corner there was an old rocking chair. The strange thing was that everything in that room was covered with dust except the rocking chair.

I found the door and slowly pulled it open. There was only a big open space. I stepped in, and the door closed behind me. I screamed for my wife, but she didn't come. I started looking for another way out, but then I realized there were no windows, nor doors. I turned around to try the room door again, but it was gone. I didn't understand what was going on. I had just seen the house from the outside, and there were windows on all sides. Everything started to blur, and the next thing I remember is waking up on the old dust floor. I stood up in the room that now had two windows and a front door.

I ran outside to my Ford pickup truck; my wife was still inside. I opened the door, and I asked her how long I had been gone. She replied with "maybe five minutes at the most. " It felt like it had been hours. I jumped in my truck and went home. The next morning when I walked out my front door my flashlight (I had left it at the haunted home) was lying at my feet with a card next to it. It read "don't return. " That's was the scariest day of my life man.

Submitted by Lee Lynn, Ozark, Alabama

55.
A Tale From Gray Court
Gray Court, South Carolina

I grew up in Gray Court, SC. Ever since I was a small child I've experienced paranormal things. My family owns land off of Main Street in Gray Court, and once owned the brick house in the front of the property that once used to be the Gray estate back before the Civil War. I've seen all kinds of things such as orbs floating in mid air to hearing people talking like they were in the walls. I and other family members have seen these ghosts of people before.

One story that always sticks with me is a cool night my husband was outside working on our car behind our house, and he was pushed by something that I could not see. However, you could tell that he was shoved off his feet. His being from Cuba he knows of Voodoo and all, and he was terrified. He told me that he felt a very cold feeling and anger when it happened. He demanded we go inside. Later that night I was walking through the living room when I felt coldness and looked into the window in my kitchen when I saw an older man's face in the glass. It was gray and very scary, looking at me, and before I could scream he was gone. That was just one night that myself and my husband will never forget.. I have many more tales of ghost sightings in Gray Court, SC.

Submitted by Michelle, Gray Court, South Carolina

. . . .

56.
Bloody Battle Of Indian Rock
Salina, Kansas

I moved to Salina after I graduated from high school and lived there from the mid 80s to early 90s. The last two years I lived there, I lived by myself in an apartment across the street north of Indian Rock Park. There were two bedrooms in that apartment, both on the second floor, one on the north side and one on the south side. I slept in the one on the south side.

One night I awoke to something on my bed. It was as if someone was jumping on my bed, alternating from left leg to right leg, and it was moving back and forth very quickly, almost in a violent nature. I wondered if I was dreaming, but I could clearly see the bed move. I was terrified, in shock, and couldn't move. Almost as quickly as it began, it quit. I just lay there for the longest time with my eyes open, being afraid to go back to sleep.

After that I slept in the north bedroom. I had a difficult time going to sleep, as I just couldn't shake off what had happened. Some time after I began sleeping in the north bedroom, I started having horrible, horrible nightmares. I would be dreaming of something that felt very bad, as if someone was trying to torture someone. Even in my dream state, I would be telling myself I needed to wake up, and I would . . . But into another dream, and then into another dream before I could actually wake up, kind of like I was trapped. I was very thankful when I finally moved from that apartment and out of Salina.

Sometime maybe around 2007 or so I learned of the Battle of Indian Rock and that it was a very bloody battle. I got chills, remembering my experience, and wondered at that time if what I had experienced years before was an angry spirit from that battle.

Submitted by Michele, Salina, Kansas

57.
Who Are Those People?
Smyrna, Tennessee

We have lived in Smyrna for about one a half years and are renting a house near the West Fork Subdivision. We've had random stuff happening since we moved in. However, the activity has increased over the past two to three months. I believe the house was built in 2007. Within the first six months, our two older daughters were face-timing their friends (not at the same time, different occasions, and about five different people) in our room lying on our bed with their friend's camera view facing our bathroom that's attached to our room. Each of those friends would ask "who is that behind you?" Our daughter would be telling their friends "no one. " Being a little freaked out, they thought their friends were messing around.

On the last face-time session in our room another friend asked "who is that man behind you?" She quickly turned around as she was saying "no one," then they said "well, they're gone now!" She ran out of the room and told us what happened. My two daughters never shared with each other what their friends claimed seeing until then. After that my oldest daughter heard someone call her name on two different occasions and would reply "yeah?" quickly realizing it wasn't or didn't even sound like us. In the past two to three months we have experienced my other daughter being shushed when no one else was around her, and she wasn't even talking, I've been scratched and touched. My husband's air supply was cut off from his sleep apnea machine, and he has seen some kind of energy ball floating in the middle of the kitchen about a size of a cantaloupe. We have been angrier towards one another. We all get strong feelings that we're being watched, or that someone is standing next to us when we are the only one in the room or the only one home.

I'm sure there are many other things but can't think of it all right now, or was just over looked. We have thought and tried everything we can think of to come up with explanations or reasons of how these things could have happened. However, we are clueless and don't think we are the only ones in this house. I am not sure if it's the land that's being haunted or what because no one has died who has lived in this house.

Submitted by Anonymous, Smyrna, Tennessee

. . . .

58.
The Yellow House
Lowell, Massachusetts

I used to own a house on Lawrence Street South Lowell. When I first moved in one of the kids in the neighborhood said "Oh you live in the Haunted House. " I didn't think anything of it at the time. My daughter was little at the time and never wanted to go to bed. I did not think anything of it at the time, more on that later. Well we used to hear things at night (no big deal.) Lights were found on (I thought someone had come downstairs and left it on. One morning we came downstairs and found the large painting that was hanging on the living room wall on the floor against the wall. The spike that was holding the painting on the wall was intact. The wire on the back of the painting was intact. No way had this fallen off the wall. Besides we did not hear it fall. That finally made me start to think, and I remembered what the little kid next door had said to me.

Different things continued to occur though nothing harmful or destructive. One night my then wife and I were sleeping in bed upstairs. I got up to go to the bathroom. When I came out I saw who I thought was my wife in the dark with the same height and same length of long hair. I said I didn't know you were up. No reply. She went down the stairs, did not say anything. As I walked past, I got to the bedroom, and my wife was asleep in bed. I knew then I had seen the ghost. I NEVER believed in anything like ghosts or supernatural in any way prior to that night.

My daughter who was about five years old at that time told me a couple of years ago when the subject came up in conversation. She said "dad, why do you think I didn't want to go to bed. I wasn't being a brat I was afraid of the ghost. " The house was sold in the 80s we lived there from 75 to the early 80s. I just wonder if someone died tragically in that house. I do not want to give the address in respect of the people who live there now, but at the time I lived there the house was green, and is now yellow.

Submitted by Rich, Lowell, Massachusetts

. . . .

59.
South End Of Newton
Newton, North Carolina

I grew up in the south end of Newton, just a couple of roads up from the elementary school. The one-bedroom apartment my mother rented was an old two-story house that had been divided into three separate apartments: one upstairs and two downstairs with three separate doors exiting on the front porch. The first strange things I can remember as a kid was having an extremely uneasy feeling while being alone in the bathroom. It was almost like being watched even with the door closed. My mother for years would hear what sounded like marbles rolling while she was in the closet. She just assumed it was the older neighbor messing around with something on her side. However, when the woman died some years later the noise continued and eventually got to where I would hear it as well.

My mother woke up one night from a dead sleep and saw a head (no body or legs) floating across the bedroom into the kitchen area. My brother, who is twelve years older than me, waited to tell me this until I was a little older. Mom was at work one night, and he and myself were sleeping when his bed started shaking violently. The walls of the room (we all shared a bedroom) turned red and then like a switch had been flipped off. His bed stopped shaking, and the walls went back to normal. I had a good friend spend the night one time, and he slept on the couch in the living room. The next morning he was awaken by talking coming from the kitchen. He assumed I was awake, so he got up to join me. When he stepped through the doorway into the kitchen area the talking just stopped, and no one was in there. He walked into our bedroom, and we were still out cold. That was the last time he stayed over.

I experienced a tall and very black shadow moving through the doorway in the bedroom one evening around 3:00, while I was home alone getting ready for football practice. Hitting ice cold spots in the air while walking down the hall, and seeing things just inside of your peripheral vision move were just the everyday normal in that house. We moved after living there twelve years or so, and with that all of the stuff stopped happening.

Submitted by , Newton, North Carolina

. . . .

60.
Ghost Story of Ft. Riley
Fort Riley, Kansas

I was with the Air Defense Artillery at Ft. Riley between late 1993 to March of 1996. Once in the field in the northern training areas out by Keats Gate, I was a driver for a Bradley Stinger Vehicle and was on guard duty between the hours of midnight and 0200. Our vehicle was in protected position where only the main gun is visible from the hole. I was looking through the infrared vision and poking up through the hatch to check things out. I ended up resting my chin on the lip of the hatch and just looking out at the tall grass blowing in the cold wind quite so quite.

I then remember it getting extremely cold as I heard horses at a gallop. I looked to my east as I was facing northeast, and I saw three Cav. Soldiers on horseback in "Custer" era uniform. When the lead soldier with sergeant stripes got off his horse and turned to the other two. (Now think I'm guessing at this time I'm approx. 125m. away from them and can hear him clear as a bell like he's directly in front me.) He said to them "SHHHHHH walk your horses quietly for that soldier is sleeping," and he slowly turned and reached his arm with an out pointed finger pointing directly at me. I snapped up and realized I've been asleep, and it was just so cold that I could see my breath. I closed that hatch and didn't come out until my T. C. woke up and took over guard duty.

A few weeks later I was renting a room at the on post inn because my wife was finally joining me at Ft. Riley. While there I was reading the in-room three ring binder and saw a tab that read "Ghost Stories of Ft. Riley. " Intrigued, I flipped to the page and read the story of the three riders on the parade field. I get goose bumps to this day, and this was all in the year 1994. I really don't believe it's the same soldiers from the parade field. Isn't one of them a L.T. or something? Anyway hope y'all enjoy. I also have a few more stories from Ft. Leonard Wood in Mo., but another time.

Submitted by J, Fort Riley, Kansas

. . . .

61.
We Only Stayed Three Days
Ingleside, Texas

I was about five when I lived in a house on West Main Street. I'm pretty sure it's boarded up now. But it's a white one-story house with an attic that's been upturned into room. My family moved in one day and we only stayed for three days before moving out. The first occurrences happened in the bedroom me and my baby sister shared (she was still in a crib.) I would repeatedly see a black entity or shadow not even in the shape of a human in the corner of the room. I told my mother the room was scary, and I didn't want to stay in there. It sort of freaked her out when I told her what I saw, and she brought up with my father. My father doesn't believe any of the paranormal so he brushed it off right away. My mother however definitely believes in spirits and energies, and she noticed that the feeling she got from the house was uncomfortable.

As for the night that finally made us move out. I was sleeping that night in my bare bedroom (in the process of being unpacked) with my sister's bed and my bed. I woke up to my bed shaking, the kind of shaking from a person grabbing the metal frame and pushing and pulling. I was curious and looked under my bed to see what was happening. What I saw was a human looking figure, except it was completely black like smoke. When I looked at its face it was turned sideways towards me with only eyes. The eyes were glowing red, and this black entity started growling like a wolf. To this day I still have nightmares, and I'm running away as fast as I could to my parents with the fear of death. I then ran in crying to my mother. This wasn't the only thing though.

My parents were having their own encounter the same time as me. My mother was the first to wake up with a very uncomfortable feeling, like something was watching. She got up and was chilled. She had goose bumps, and the hairs were rising on her neck. The dog we have was running in and going crazy. She was barking and being aggressive like she never has before. My mom watched her and noticed she was running around in a pattern: first to below the attic door with the pull down steps then to the basement door. Finally she would be back to the bedroom and repeated. Naturally my mother was scared. She turned back to where my father was. He then woke up yelling and choking, saying someone was trying to kill him. He said he felt hands around his neck, and he couldn't breathe. After that was when I came into the room crying.

My mother, finally with support from my father, started packing what we got out and moved us out of there. This happened in three days. I would say this spirit is definitely angry and does not want anyone there. I did do some research, and the house was built in 1940 and is currently trying to be sold (seems quite desperately too). From the pictures it is currently boarded up.

Submitted by Eliza, Ingleside, Texas

. . . .

62.
Pressler Grove
Fort Knox, Kentucky

First off, I was a huge skeptic of anything paranormal... But not now! I lived on-base at Pressler Grove for a little less than two years. When we first moved in our neighbors warned us about "ghostly activity" and other weird phenomena that would occur during the night, especially between 2-3 am. I thought nothing of this and wrote it off, though I did notice the heavy footsteps you would hear nightly going down our hall. I wrote it off as our neighbors' and the houses in Pressler Grove are connected. Then the neighbors PCS'd, and there was almost a year of no one living next door. That's when the activity really picked up.

One day as I was doing laundry in the basement I heard heavy breathing over my right shoulder. When I turned around there was a dark apparition with red eyes staring at me from the corner of the basement. I freaked out and ran upstairs. I told a neighbor what happened, and he contacted the Louisville Paranormal Society. They came out and ran an investigation that weekend and caught on video a child-shaped shadow figure walking down the hall and into our bedroom, amongst many other things. Way too many things happened in that house to write, but here are some highlights: lamps moving across tables, lights turning out simultaneously (on different outlets,) shadows dashing up the stairwell, TV's turning off, an entity jumping on my wife while she was sleeping, three knocks on the floor coming from the basement. The worst was the whispering sounds of my name when I was alone at night. DO NOT move into Pressler Grove unless you are single and prepared to deal with some craziness. These spirits will ruin your marriage, as they did mine and countless others around me.

Submitted by Jason, Fort Knox, Kentucky
. . . .

63.
Mysterious Force
Danvers, Massachusetts

I'm not sure if this constitutes as a sighting or not, but I thought maybe I should at least document it since it was a rather chilling experience. I was walking my dog up at the Rebecca Nurse House and have been doing this for about two years now. I rent an apartment on Sylvan Street, and the homestead is just a short walk away. Well, I was walking my dog Henry up by the cemetery when all of a sudden a tremendous feeling of fear came over me. I was shaking like a child and could not control my body.

Now what made this even stranger was that Henry was acting really strange as well. He was whining and moving back and forth and then into a circular, almost chasing his tail sort of pattern. Now what happened next I can neither confirm nor deny whether it was a supernatural force or natural force, but "something" with great force pushed me to the ground. It was with such force that it knocked me unconscious for what seemed a while but was probably only a minute or two. After this I stood up and grabbed Henry's leash and walked home extremely disoriented. I haven't been back there since then but would like to visit again.

Submitted by Shane, Danvers, Massachusetts

. . . .

64.
A House In Warwick
Warwick, Rhode Island

My husband and I lived in a house in Warwick that was very active to say the least. We lived there for 17 years. So many things went on, and I always felt that there was more than one spirit. I also believe that there was a portal in that house. This house was featured on Ghost Hunters way back in 2007. It was originally investigated in September 2006 and aired in 2007. Anyway, some of the things I can say in one word or two were banging sounds, children running and playing in the living room, footsteps, voices, toys constantly going on, seeing shadows, my son seeing "people," and our dog acting like she was seeing something. I would have dreams constantly of dead relatives or family friends that would give me messages or sometimes not. I had nightmares and was seeing the blackest of black in my bedroom at night. Our lights were continuously blowing out or going dim and then going very bright.

I always had the feeling like something was watching me. We had strange and creepy voices on the background of people calling my answering machine. (You could hear behind the message a very creepy negative spirit swearing at me in a hush tone.) There were cold drafts (not from windows or doors), items being moved, and more importantly, troublemaking within my family. I loved that house but realized we needed to move because something inside me just told me it's time to go.

We moved about five years ago and can't believe how different the "air" is here. How much lighter and how much better we sleep! Our sleep was constantly disturbed in the middle of the night at the house in Warwick. One of my sons and I were the ones who saw, heard, and felt things the most. My husband, having an electrical engineering background, would investigate to see if there were logical explanations. To his surprise, he saw something that he could not explain. It shook him up, to say the least. I still get some "oddities" here at this house, but I feel it is calmer. The energy is better and lighter. Thanks for reading!

Submitted by Lynn, Warwick, Rhode Island

. . . .

65.
Alice
Springfield, Ohio

I grew up in a house on E. Cecil Street. I lived there for almost eleven years. There was a lot of activity in that house. It was haunted by a little girl we called Alice. We called her Alice because when my nephew was about two years old he was chasing an unknown apparition and told her "stop Alice!" I have seen her many times. She was a young girl about eight or nine years old, dressed in late 1800 early 1900 clothing. I think everyone has seen her that lived in that house. She really didn't bother anyone unless you stated you didn't believe in ghosts, and by the time you left my house you did.

Also, in that house, I believe there was something evil in the basement. There was a really dark corner in the basement. No matter what light source you put down in the basement, that part of the basement never lit up. I always felt like something was watching me and would attack me when I was down there. I hated being down there any longer than I had to be. Some of the activities we experienced there was one time we were all in the living room talking, and all of a sudden the TV remote did a complete 360, and the TV came on, with no one near it. We found our cordless phones in the attic, where no one ever went.

There are a lot more stories. The thing I find odd is that since my family has moved out, I have never seen anyone live there for more than a year. It has been about twelve years since my family has moved out of there. I would like to do some research on the property, but I never have time when I go home to visit.

Submitted by Jen, Springfield, Ohio
. . . .

66.
Old Voodoo
New Iberia, Louisiana

A house on S. Fulton Street is haunted. My family and I lived there for six months. Things started slow like footsteps, hearing voices, things moving, doors opening, lights coming on, etc. About five months in things got serious. One night I came in from outside, walked through the kitchen to my room, and passed the bathroom door.

Out of the corner of my eye I saw someone standing in the bathroom, but I didn't think anything of it. When I came back through the bathroom the door was still open. I thought maybe it was my daughter wanting to use it. I went through the bathroom into the girl's room, and my daughter was on her bed almost asleep. I asked if she was up, and she said "no. " I freaked out because the girl I saw was wearing something from the 1970s.

About a week later my oldest daughter and I were in the kitchen fixing dinner when all the sudden the spice rack flew off the wall. We just stood there thinking "what just happened?" We did an EVP one night and caught something jumping off the girl's bed to the floor and running into the boy's room. One night I was dead asleep, and all the sudden I felt like I got slammed in the side of the head and woke up to blood running down my face. Something had split my ear. I started getting wakened up in the middle of the night to what felt like my arms and legs getting tugged on.

Right before we moved we were all in the kitchen fixing dinner, and all the sudden a very loud bang and the stove had been slammed and shoved over. We all freaked out staring at the stove. Then a cup by the sink flew off the counter. When we were freaking out over the cup something was trying to slide our dinner off the stove. The house in the last month got scary as hell. We later found out that a couple of old women from Germany were doing Voodoo and other summoning stuff in the house.

Submitted by DK, New Iberia, Louisiana
. . . .

67.
The Cumberland Area
Cumberland, Maryland

I have lived in the Cumberland area my whole life. My first experience with the paranormal was in the house I grew up in on Avirett Avenue. The house was built in 1920. When I was a young child ages 2-6 I was plagued with demonic scary dreams I have never been able to put into words. I always had feelings I was being watched, but the only ghost I ever saw was in that house when I was at age 8. I got ready for my day at 4th grade, and I came downstairs. A man in early 1900s clothing was standing there. I couldn't even look at him. I just ran to the kitchen and begged the specter not to hurt me. The man looked exactly like a photo of my great grandfather, but why he would be at our house I don't know.

Fast forward to after I left home. The first place I stayed was a house that had been put into apartments on Braddock Road closer to the Lavale side. Several times my boyfriend and I witnessed shadow footprints passing outside our bedroom door like someone was in the hallway. One day I was in the apartment alone in the bedroom, and my boyfriend had the US flag and an Army flag on his wall. The heater was not on, and no drafts were in the room at all. However, the US flag was flapping like as if it was in the wind. The army flag was not moving. I always had a strong feeling it was the spirit of a soldier. It's well known that Braddock Road was used as a path for soldiers, but who knows?

The scariest experiences or feelings I had was at a house on Williams Road on Irons Mountain. My boyfriend rented the house out with several of his friends. It had been unoccupied for fifteen years. My boyfriend was excited to show me the house, but when we arrived as soon as I looked at the house I had a terrible feeling. I didn't want to go inside, and everyone else thought I was being stuck up. My boyfriend said I could have at least pretended I liked

124

it, but it scared me. I never felt like that before. Shortly after they moved in the entire side of the house was covered with thousands of flies like something straight out of a horror film.

I am sensitive to paranormal activity, and I experienced more than any other person there. One night I drove nearly an hour just to see my boyfriend only to turn around and leave because of the malevolent presence, and it started stealing my photos. Eventually I researched how to make it go away, and I burned sage and walked through the house. I told the spirits to find the light and move on. After that I was able to be in the house, and eventually everyone's bad feelings went away. That was six years ago, and I haven't had an experience since then probably because I stopped paying attention.

Submitted by Laura, Cumberland, Maryland

. . . .

68.
The Open House
South Mills, North Carolina

I went into the house on Nosay Road when they had an open house. I was alone. I left the crowd. I went upstairs to the attic. On the wall there were three names closer to the floor as if someone was sitting and writing their name as to be remembered. One name appeared to be a woman by the name of Abigail, and beside the name I saw 1958. I was looking around the attic, and I found myself feeling heaviness and a feeling that a million eyes were watching me. I was not going to let that bother me, so I said out loud "I come in peace. " As soon as I finished saying that, I was standing at what appeared to be a different part of the attic. All of a sudden I heard the most ear piercing whistle I have ever heard. I knew that was not a friendly gesture to stay. I started to feel disoriented and knew I had to leave.

As I ran down the steps to leave the house; everybody else was gone. I separated myself from the crowd of onlookers and to my surprise I finally understood that I do have a special gift of knowing what I already knew to be the truth. That house has been harboring secrets of the past. As long as I have lived here there have been numerous occupants. My son went to school with a friend that lived there, and he invited my son to spend the night, but my son declined because his friend told him stories of things his family experienced while living in that home. I was able to tell my son that everything he has been told about that house is true.

My only question is "was there more turmoil in that house than we will ever know?" If I ever have the chance to go back in that house, I will, because I do know for a fact that what I already knew should be properly investigated. So if that chance ever comes my way again, I will be ready to prove my experience was truth. The day of the open house there was more curiosity in most of the people that are in search of the same thing I have been for

126

years and years, not that they really wanted to buy the house. This is my story, and it is all truth.

Submitted by SLM, South Mills, North Carolina

. . . .

69.
The Man in the Window
Newman, California

When I was a little girl my mother, sisters, and brother lived in an old house at the corner of Main and Tulare Streets. There was an old man named Mr. Lawrencen who owned the house, and his shop was in the same lot. I believe there is now a drug store there. So many terrifying things happened in this house when I was five to eight years old. At night when we were sleeping someone would pull my hair. My mom would yell at us to turn the TV off because she could hear people laughing and talking when the TV was not on. Doors would close on their own. I sometimes felt like someone was suffocating me when I slept.

One very late night my sister walked into a bedroom to get to the bathroom. No one slept in this room because we were afraid. She saw an illuminated man with his hand pressed up against the window from the outside looking into the room. This house had a high foundation (not possible for someone to stand outside and look in unless there was a ladder. My mom got scared and gathered us up, and we walked down Main Street all the way to my grandmother's house at the other end of Main Street. As we walked out the front door, we all looked back and could see what looked like flames in front of the window. Other terrifying experiences occurred. I guess I should write a book. I don't know who lived there before us, but it would be interesting to know. We lived there from 1962 to 1965.

Submitted by Helen, Newman, California

. . . .

70.
Two Soldiers
Staunton, Virginia

I lived on Thornrose Avenue in Staunton almost 17 years ago. We were across the street from the cemetery. I often had encounters with the spirits of at least two soldiers, one Union and one Confederate. The Union soldier I would often see standing in the doorway to my bathroom as I lounged in an old cast iron claw foot tub on the second floor. I would have my head back, almost upside down out of the tub, and would see him standing behind me. Also there was a HUGE amount of tension between the soldiers, as if they were STILL at war all these years later.

On two separate occasions I felt hands around my throat while I was sitting on the toilet. I would open my eyes and see a face on the wall next to me, almost growling. Then, the Union soldier would pass through that same wall in front of me, and the tension around my throat would release instantly. It was like he was there to watch over me. It didn't really surprise me to have these experiences being so close to Thornrose Cemetery where there are reportedly over 1700 soldiers buried there. It was also probably in an area of battles of the Civil War.

Submitted by Melissa, Staunton, Virginia

. . . .

71.
Not Friendly
Coarsegold, California

My mother has lived in the Yosemite Springs Park for the past thirty years, and when my kids were young they always found Indian artifacts around her home. Sometime in 2008 to 2009 my mom moved to a beautiful little home set up on a hill, and the house was in a wooded area with a backyard garden and many trees. The rent was really cheap for such a beautiful home, and we were excited at our luck in finding it.

Shortly after mom moved in, one night she was watching TV she suddenly heard pounding on the outside of her house. It was as if someone was trying to get in. She went outside to check and found nothing. This continued for the next several weeks with mom calling security only for them to say there was nothing.

One night mom forgot her cell phone in her car, so she walked out to the garage to get her purse which was in the trunk. She opened the garage door, and as she was retrieving the phone, without notice, the garage door came down on her. As she started to fall, she twisted to catch herself on the bench, so she fell in a twisted manner fracturing her femur. She could not explain to us what had happened, and the garage opener was working fine when we checked it.

Following her hospitalization, she returned to the house. The very first night she was home the noises returned, but they were now inside the house. First it was a pounding on the wall above her bed and then a rustling of things on her dresser. She moved to the guest room, and the noises followed. We called exterminator, and they found nothing. She put a blanket on the floor with food in the middle thinking it was some sort of rodent, and nothing.

The noises continued. Because my mom is a religious person, she refuses to accept that this could be a ghost, but after several weeks of this torment she moved. Interestingly, when she gave her notice the landlord was very sad and said she has never been able to keep a renter for more than three months. It is pretty obvious to me that this house was built in the middle of an Indian burial ground, and the ghosts are not friendly. To this day, my mom refuses to talk about what happened in that house. Weird.

Submitted by Anonymous, Coarsegold, California

. . . .

72.
Wrecking Ghost
Saint Anthony, Indiana

Rack up another car wreck for the bridge ghost. A man and his family were forced off the road by something he didn't know what it was. He was more scared of people thinking him crazy so he said something Silver ran him off the road and shut up. Everyone there knows about the ghost of the bridge. He didn't need to worry. Everyone that stopped there was thinking the same thing. The policemen got out of the car and said "looks like the ghost got another one. " The man's jaw dropped, and we all laughed. The police men said "we work wrecks at this bridge two or three times a year. We'll just put it down as something run you off the road. "

The owner of the land the bridge sets on came, and someone jokingly hollered "you ought to get an exorcist down here. " He hollered back "from what I heard that's how we got it in the first place. Hell, it never did me no harm, and I ain't gonna do nothing to make it start. " We all had a good laugh. Some did get scared and left, but it didn't bother the rest. This was the first time I got to be there for one of the ghost shows. The people came trying to see the ghost, but whatever it was, was long gone.

Submitted by Terry, Saint Anthony, Indiana

. . . .

73.
On Downing Street
Greensboro, North Carolina

Our home on Downing Street was nightmare for my family and me. In the Fall of 1976 poltergeist activity seemed to be focused on me when I was eleven years old, and my sister was fifteen. My bed would shake at night, and sheets were often suddenly pulled off my bed. My sister often would awake to feeling her hand held by what seemed to be an old woman. My mother was awaken once by her foot being shaken. Even our family dog seemed to be trouble and would growl at unseen presences at night. Odd smell of perfume which my sister said smelled like 'old lady stuff' filled the air. Door in the house often open and closed without explanation, and I had strange dreams of often feeling myself levitated and floating through a woods behind our house that lead to a cemetery.

The house was blessed by a priest from Saint Pius, but the blessing only knocked off the poltergeist activity for about a week. Often at night I would awake to my sheets being suddenly yanked off and even had a scary and a bit embarrassing experience when sleeping face down and having my underwear suddenly yanked off. Odd smells often would occur during the day. We heard the sound in another room of something having fallen but nothing to be seen. I have no real explanation for much of this other than many young friends of mine often played in a cemetery behind the woods behind our house at Westminster. Maybe something attached itself to us. We also had dabbled in a lot of things we should not have and collected lots of horror comics which we traded along with a large stash of magazines which probably made us some sort of Orgone magnets. Fortunately, the whole episode was over in about four to five months and was gone by the spring of 1977.

The old house still stands though our family moved out of it some 29 years ago. I would be interested in knowing if anyone has experienced anything or anyone in the Downing Street area has any similar experiences.

Submitted by Jim, Greensboro, North Carolina

. . . .

74.
Haunted House on 711
Powhatan, Virginia

My wife and I lived in a house on HWY 711 for a year. It's right
by Sublets Tavern. My wife and I went to a yard sale and come to
find out the people who had the yard sale actually lived in that
house. We just had small talk and bought a few things for the
kids. Before we left she said, "Have you heard it?"

I had no clue what she was talking about, so I said "the voices and
banging. " I told her no and got in the car as fast as I could. I
figured she was crazy or on drugs, so my wife and I left.

A few months go by, and nothing happens. I forgot about it to be
honest. I was packing and preparing for a work trip in CA. I took
a break and was watching TV, and there were these thunderous
bangs from upstairs. It sounded like a herd of cattle running up
and down the stairs and upstairs.

Then over the weeks it started to escalate. I heard my son's name
called out by a man. I had a clock that had not worked in years,
but every time my wife would pass it, it would start clicking and
gonging.

I could go on and on and probably write a book on it there were so
many things that happened. Come to find out when we were
moving, everyone in that area of Powhatan knew it was haunted.

Submitted by Hwy 711, Powhatan, Virginia

. . . .

75.
Took Us A While
Grayson, Kentucky

In August of 2014 I started to attend Kentucky Christian University in Grayson. I started out living in Waters Hall, where the football team lived. Well I made a friend named Nathan, who lived in the apartments on campus with his wife and at the time six months old son. After a while I started to live with them. For a while nothing weird happened. Then we started to hear things and see things, but we dismissed it as we were sleep deprived because we're college kids. Well one night they laid the baby down to go to sleep about 8:00 pm, and every hour on the hour until 2:00 am he would wake up screaming in terror.

When he finally went to sleep, so did we. About 4:00 am I got up to use the restroom that was across the hall from the baby's room. As I walked by the room I could hear what sounded like someone soothing a baby, but the door was shut, and the light was off. I opened the door, turned the light on, and the baby was nowhere to be found. I thought he woke up again, and they took him into their room. Well, the next morning the baby was in its crib, and the door was open. My friend came out and asked if I had opened the door. I told him what happened during the night. He thought I was crazy because the baby was "in his room all night. "

After that they took the baby to stay with the grandparents, and the next day things started to get weird. Doors were opening and closing by themselves. Weird noises were coming from the baby's room, so my friend called a guy who told us to try and provoke it with Bibles. As my friend was reaching to get his Bible out of his room, the door slammed shut. We decided we weren't going to stay there that night. The next day as we were getting out of class, my friend's wife called him freaked out, so we went back to the apartment. She told us the silverware drawer opened up and silverware started to move on its own, so we decided we weren't

136

coming back. My friend went to get the paper work, and the woman over the apartment asked why, and he told her. She said "I'm surprised it took you this long to figure it out. " To this day we still don't know what she meant by that, and we don't really want to know.

Submitted by Cory, Grayson, Kentucky

. . . .

76.
Spirit At work
Gardena, California

One night I was in the middle of a dream that I was telling my husband that we had a spirit in the house that was going to set off the smoke detectors, when a second later the smoke detector went off and scared us both half to death! The next morning my husband went into the room with the smoke detector that had gone off, and he found that the battery had been pulled out. The ceiling in that room is a good seven feet high, so you would need a ladder to reach it, and neither of us had even been in that room for a couple of days. Once in a while they still go off at random.

We figured it's probably the ghost that plays short riffs of electric guitar music. The first couple of times I heard it I figured it was coming from an electronic game, but when I finally asked my husband what he was playing it turned out he wasn't playing a game at all! I asked where the music was coming from, and he said 'what music?' I was the only one who had heard it, so we figured there had to be more spirit activity at work!

Submitted by Deanna, Gardena, California

. . . .

77.
Creepy Feeling
Spring, Texas

We have lived in Timberlane for ten years. From the time we moved in, we have experienced a man-shaped figure that walks back and forth across the entrance to the kitchen. It has never done anything threatening. It is just very disconcerting, especially for guests who know nothing of the phenomena.

My daughter has had disturbing occurrences, including someone leaning over and whispering in her ear, "get up" while she was in bed. One day she was standing in front of a darkened hallway one day, posing for a selfie. The facial recognition feature on her iPhone picked up her face, and then picked up a smaller face in back of her in the hallway. She was startled and turned around to see if someone was in the hallway. No one was there, and when she turned around a rush of cold air hit her.

Also one night we had a friend staying in the downstairs bedroom. She was in the bed and looked over at the LED clock on the nightstand and checked the time. A little while later as she was dozing she looked over again to check it, and something was blocking the view of the clock. She felt someone sitting on the edge of the bed, and assuming that it was my daughter, she began talking to her. When she got no answer she started to freak out. She texted my daughter, and my daughter came downstairs to check on her. Needless to say, she couldn't wait to leave.

Another night another of my daughter's friends came over and while sitting in the upstairs living area, saw a man follow my daughter into the kitchen. Upon being told that my husband was asleep and there was no one else in the house, she freaked out and didn't want to come back for a long time. Several of my daughter's friends have come over to pick her up and would not come in. They have said that they have a bad feeling about the house.

I personally have never had a threatening experience in the house, although it is creepy as hell and you definitely don't want to be here alone!

Submitted by Liz, Spring, Texas

. . . .

78.
Time To Move
Santa Barbara, California

I lived in an apartment on Cota Street. That was VERY haunted! I'd be in my room and would think I was hearing my roommates come in the door and be doing stuff in the kitchen, but by the time I would come out, there was no one there. On Halloween one of my roommates left for a party about forty minutes away, and twenty minutes after he left I was in my room. I heard the front door open, so I hollered 'hey Chris, can you make sure I turned the oven off?' There was no answer. I asked both of my roommates later if they ever heard noise like that from the neighbor's unit, and they said "not really. " When I told them about hearing the door open and someone in the kitchen they looked at each other and said this whole time they'd been experiencing the same thing.

My closet door would often creak open in the middle of the night. I kept thinking it was just because I'd left something too close to the hinge. However, one night I woke up to my dresser drawers slamming open and shut. At first I thought I was having a nightmare, but I shouted 'whoever or whatever you are, leave now! You're scaring me, and you don't belong here!' Just like that, the commotion stopped. A couple of days later I asked my other roommate if he'd ever heard or seen anything strange around there, and he said that one night he woke up, and his usually really warm room was like an icebox. That was when he looked in the corner, and he saw the figure of a man pointing at him. I told him what I'd experienced, and we all decided it was time to move!

Submitted by Sally, Santa Barbara, California

. . . .

79.
Friendly Soldier
Fort Scott, Kansas

My niece was on a field trip there and said she and her class had a very nice conversation with a tour guide who was "pretending" to be a Civil War soldier and was wearing a Civil War costume. I assumed she was talking about an actor who was dressed up for the field trip. Since my niece was so excited about that field trip I decided to bring her up to the fort again, so I could hopefully meet the gentleman who she met that day.

After talking to some other tour guides we found out that there was no actor or anyone else dressed up as a soldier the day of the trip. We also found out that since it was a field trip the fort was closed to any other visitors except the teachers, principals, and students. That was when I talked to some managers, and they told me that many other visitors had reported having the exact same experience with a male soldier from the Civil War.

It wasn't long after that that we concluded that the person that my niece, her class, and her teacher had talked to was the ghost of a friendly Civil War soldier who had accidently shot himself near the area where the teacher said that they had the conversation. After that I will never go to the fort ever again, let alone let my niece go there!

Submitted by Angel, Fort Scott, Kansas

. . . .

80.
Lonely Innocent Soul
Fort Wayne, Indiana

Fort Wayne is the second largest city in Indiana, and one of its main thoroughfares is North Anthony Boulevard, a beautiful, tree lined street that runs north and south. Most of the homes in that particular area of town are near the century old mark, its original inhabitants long gone. When I was in my early twenties I lived in one of the homes on that street for several months. The house was full of character, and naturally being an older home it made its share of bumps and noises, boards creaking, etc. At first, I didn't think much of the many noises and strange things that were going on in the home, but as time went on it seemed as though the house itself was crying for attention.

One night we were all sitting downstairs in the living room watching TV when suddenly the upstairs shower came on and the sound of somebody taking a shower. We all looked at each other as if we had just seen a ghost, but we knew that no one was on the second floor at that time, so we just tried to ignore what happened. Several days later I was down in the basement, which was more like a cellar, when I felt a small cold hand gently tug at the back side of my arm. I spared no time getting out of that creepy old basement. As I was running up the stairs, I thought I heard the sound of a child's laughter behind me. I wasn't the only one experiencing strange things in that old house. My best friend's five-year-old daughter was seen talking and interacting with someone or something invisible. When we asked her who she was talking to, she said it was the "other" little girl who was waiting for her mommy to come get her.

One fall afternoon I was upstairs on the second floor cleaning when I heard the distinct sound of footsteps coming up the stairs. As the footsteps got closer and closer, suddenly they stopped. When I looked out into the hallway, there was not a soul in sight.

At that point, I was scared to death; I ran out of the house and called my dad to come pick me up until everyone got home from work. I was not staying another minute in this house by myself and within a week I moved out of the home. Several months later, on a hunch, I decided to do a little bit of research on the house. I learned that shortly after the house was built, a five-year-old child was hit and killed by a drunk driver while playing with her dolls in the front yard. Shortly after, the grieving parents packed up the house and moved to another town, which explains the lonely innocent soul left behind, still looking and waiting for her mother to return home and collect her. I pray that she has found peace in the loving arms of her mother and can finally rest in peace.

Submitted by Mary, Fort Wayne, Indiana

. . . .

81.
The Giggling Sounds
Cannelton, Indiana

In November 2005 I was recently divorced and starting a new chapter in my life with my five-year-old son. We moved out to a tiny town that shared a zipcode with Cannelton. It's called Tobinsport. There are plenty of campgrounds in Tobinsport, and it's a beautiful little country town. It is just about 6 miles north of Rocky Point marina. Anyway, I'd rented a small trailer off of a man that owned one of the campgrounds, and I'd lived there a few months. The campers went away at the end of October, and I was glad for the peace and quiet. My son got the only bedroom in the trailer, and I took the futon as my bed in the living room.

It was a little past midnight, and I'd decided to watch TV pretty late and my son had already fallen asleep. All of the sudden I heard kids giggling, little kids, more specifically little girls. I thought it was strange because summer is over! Who lets their kids out that late in the middle of November? So I went out to investigate. The campground was eerily quiet with no one in sight. Then I thought "well. maybe it's the people across the road and their kids?" So I walked to the front of the property (about a football field away.) Their house is dark, and there are still no kids. I brushed it off and went back to the trailer. Since I was still shaken I checked on my still sleeping son, and I watched TV some more. About 15 minutes later there was creepier giggling just outside. I was starting to question my sanity. When my son walked out of his room down the hallway and said "mommy I can't sleep. Those kids outside are laughing, and it bothers me. " Ok! I was done for. I told him that I would sleep with him as I met him at the end of the hallway.

Well we were going to make a mad dash for his bedroom when there was a black figure in the hallway. My son was crying because it was blocking our way, and we were both very frightened. I grabbed him in my arms and said "he can't hurt you!' and ran through the figure. We shut the door behind us. I threw my son on the bed and screamed through the door. I said "you are not welcome here! Get out of my house in the name of god! " Suddenly everything felt "lighter," and we were able to finally sleep.

Submitted by Anon, Cannelton, Indiana

. . . .

82.
Our Antique Store
Charleroi, Pennsylvania

I have an antique store located on McKean Avenue in Charleroi, Pa. My husband and I purchased it over seven years ago. The activity started off by hearing sounds like furniture being dragged across the second floor, walking, running, and tea cup being picked up and sit down. After contacting a few paranormal groups and having them provide us with evidence that the activity was real was frightening and cool at the same time. Star Radio 100.7 chose us to come to our location to have a Haunted Halloween Paranormal Investigation. So many things occurred that night to numerous people. I walked upstairs to show the girl from the group where she could set up her equipment, and in the process I received the shock of my life. I felt an icy coldness directly behind me. All of a sudden I felt arms tighten around my body. It felt as if someone was giving me a bear hug, and I instantly froze and could not speak or move. I was petrified!

When I felt the arms un-tighten from my body and felt the icy coldness move from me, I told this girl I had just been hugged. I moved quickly down the stairs and went into my office and started to cry. I was shocked, startled, and could not register what just happened to me. All of a sudden I was encountered by a psychic that the radio station brought with them. I was told a female spirit entity named Clara had just hugged me. I was blown away as this psychic knew this. It turns out that Clara was a previous owner of the Antique building we purchased, and she was dead in the building for a few weeks before she was found. Over the years there have been validated reports, photos, video, and audio evidence from customers, workers, psychics, and paranormal groups etc.

There are a few small children entities and a few male entities who have also made their presence known in the building. In a picture that was given to us by a customer there is a male's face at the top of the stairs left side under the stair rail. As recently as yesterday, I was sitting in the office at the store and clearly heard doors opening and closing. At times you will hear children running on the second floor, footsteps coming down the stairs when no one is there. Sometimes we see mists. We have learned to live amongst the spirits and the activity at the store.

Submitted by Rhonda, Charleroi, Pennsylvania

. . . .

83.
The Drum
Azusa, California

I grew up in Azusa, so I know a lot of crazy stuff happens there. We and a couple of friends lived in the little mobile home park across the road from the little restaurant where you camp. I think it was Memorial Day weekend and me and Joe decided to go down there with our fishing poles for trout. It was after midnight, and there were lots of tents around. People were sleeping, so we were trying to be as quiet as possible. We got to the edge of the campground. I mean we were whispering to each other, so we wouldn't wake anybody up.

All of a sudden we both looked at each other, and said "do you hear that?" It sounded like a drum circle. I looked around. There was nobody up, and it sounded like it was coming from across the stream and the base of the mountain, but there was no way of getting there. Right away Fat Joe who was already a superstitious person started chanting, you know like an Indian, but very low, and so did I. The drums got louder. When we stopped and opened our eyes, so did the drums. Mind you, we had our fishing lines in the water this whole time. Then boom! The trout started hitting one after another.

Submitted by Raul, Azusa, California
. . . .

84.
The Pool Table
Norwalk, California

When I was very young my parents bought a house near Alondra and Elaine. The houses on these small one way streets are pretty small and close together. As our family was growing my dad decided to make additions to the house rather than move. He added rooms and a den. He always wanted a pool table, so when the den was completed he acquired a used coin operated one that looked like it came out of a pool room or a bar. It was very heavy. It took six men to carry it in the sliding door.

I don't remember when it began, but in the evenings when we would all be sitting in the front room watching TV we would hear the cue ball getting hit and clicking with the other balls on the table. We were used to hearing this regularly, so we wouldn't pay attention at first. After a while one of my sisters or me would ask who was playing pool. It would stop of course. We would notice everyone was in the front room, and when we would check it no one would be there, and the door would be locked. My mom would make a joke about the friendly ghost who likes to play pool, so we didn't get scared.

After some time we saw markings on the floor matching the foot marks of the pool table as though it was getting move around. Remember this is the heavy table that took six men to move. It was not something that could slide over when a little girl leaned against it. There isn't really any climactic ending. When the table got sold years later it stopped. Even after we had gotten another cheap pool table, (light weight) there was no occurrences like before. This was in the 70s. There are so many other incidents of a different nature since then but not related to this specific one. Some were told to me by friends, neighbors, and relatives, but this is mine. There could be some logical scientific explanation for it all as my son would say, but that's up to the individual to decide for themselves.

Submitted by Nani, Norwalk, California

. . . .

85.
A Friendly Old Lady
New Port Richey, Florida

I am curious about any activity in the New Port Richey Library. My family and I entered, and I spotted and nodded to a very friendly black woman wearing a hat and reading a book. She appeared to be about 65-70 years old. We then passed her because we went upstairs. The next time I went in there, she was there again reading a book. She looked up at all of my children and husband and smiled at them. I was sort of puzzled why my children didn't acknowledge her friendly smile. I nodded at her and smiled.

A week or so later we were discussing the history of the library and talking about some vibes we get from it. I brought up the friendly old lady and casually mentioned her as being one of the more unusual standout patrons, just thinking my kids would say "oh, yea, her. " But they said "What old black lady?"

Nobody saw her. TWICE! I couldn't believe it. I said to my family "but we walked past her, she was so friendly, unlike most of the people on the first floor. " She smiled at each one of you. You didn't see her?!? Anyway, next time we go back, and if I see her, I will point her out. If they see her, then she is real and just a friendly person. If they don't see her, I will ask for her story and perhaps help her leave and go to source.

Submitted by A, New Port Richey, Florida

. . . .

86.
Blonde Hair In White Dress
Fenton, Michigan

We actually live in Tyrone Township, and our house is haunted by a young girl maybe around thirteen. We have heard and seen her several times. She has long blonde hair and is wearing an old fashion white plain cotton ankle length dress or nightdress. We have seen her outside our living room window, but we go outside no one is there. We also hear her laughing. My six-year-old granddaughter one day was in the living room talking with me when she was distracted and staring in the kitchen. I asked her what she was looking at, and she pointed in the kitchen and said "her. " I said "her who" because we were the only ones in the house at that time, and she said "that girl. " We see shadows move across the rooms all the time also.

My daughter saw a girl looking out our upstairs bedroom window. She thought it was me until she realized I was outside, and no one was in the house. Just last week my eight-year-old granddaughter was sitting on the couch in the living room, and my husband said that they both looked at each other at the same time. My granddaughter asked "did you hear that?" My husband said "what did you hear? And she said "a little girl laughing," but no one was there. Most recently we had all our lights go out; however, all the electrical items that were plugged in and on the same circuit breaker were still running. Just the lights all went out. The fridge, stove, heat, etc everything was working. Everyone that sees her when we asked what she looked like, they all describe her the same: the blonde hair with white dress.

Submitted by Sandy, Fenton, Michigan

. . . .

87.
Haunted Office
Wakefield, Massachusetts

In 1996-1998 I worked at the Edgewater Office Park which stands where Pleasure Island used to be on Audubon Road in Wakefield, MA. My office mates and I experienced a lot of phenomena there. We were all often touched by what felt like a coworker coming up behind us, but no one was there. One woman was plagued by swarms of gnats in her office from no identifiable source. Small objects often disappear, and once while seated in our break room the microwave suddenly came on and started flashing the word "child." Once while working alone in the office on a Sunday afternoon I looked up to see a blonde woman in pink pants and a white sweater standing in the hall. I couldn't see her face and thought she was a coworker.

I called to her at which point all of the lights and power in the office went out for about thirty seconds and came back on, and all of the office equipment started up. The fax machine began beeping a busy signal, and some of the phones started ringing. I left as soon as I could and never worked alone in the building again. After that the activity became more malevolent. Our office manager suffered a breakdown and had to leave his job and several people became inexplicably faint and ill when entering the office door. People stared feeling irritable and quarreling with each other. About this time I had enough and left!

Submitted by Vicky, Wakefield, Massachusetts

. . . .

88.
Haunted Fort Campbell
Fort Campbell, Kentucky

We lived at Fort Campbell two times, and both times it was in haunted quarters! In Pierce Village Litwin Street we kept seeing dark shadows moving in and out of the kitchen. Our son, then three-years-old, would say a mean man would talk to him at night and say to come to him. I was thrown down the stairs after feeding our baby. However, the second time, living in New Hammond Heights was worst. Right after moving in we would smell cigarette smoke, even though my husband and I never smoked. The third day after moving in, I waited for our boys to come down to eat breakfast, and I heard footsteps coming down the stairs. I spoke out loud "Mike, do you want cereal or pop tarts?" No answer, so I walked to the stairs and hollered his name. I asked "did you just come down?" He said he wasn't ready yet and still in the bathroom.

One night my husband saw a shadow going from my side of the bed to his side, and it tried to suffocate him. Many times I had three scratched lines on my body. Most times under my chest or belly. Once I wrote an address on a piece of paper with complete name and address and phone number, even how to get to her place. I could not remember why or when or who to relate it to, and I called this phone number. The young lady and I tried to figure out how or why I had her address. We phoned about three times. After that she told me her pastor advised her not to have contact with me, since there was supposed to be something wrong with this connection! I also felt being touched at night when my husband wasn't home. As strange as it sounds, all of this is true. Son's name was changed!

Submitted by Judith, Fort Campbell, Kentucky
. . . .

89.
Evil Boy
Sharon, Pennsylvania

I lived in a house on Ohio Street in Sharon for almost a year. In that year my then six-year-old daughter wouldn't enter her own bedroom day or night. She kept complaining of an old man she called "scary" that kept trying to get her to leave with him, and a little boy that wanted her to play outside at night. I shrugged off her claims as a little kid in a new house or noises from the other two apartments in the house, until I myself started hearing odd noises and seeing things that just didn't seem right. I still just ignored it, until the night I was woke up in the middle of the night to see my daughter perfectly cut off all her hair with scissors that I put in the top of my closet earlier that evening.

When I asked her why she cut her hair, she said the little boy was bugging her to go outside and play (it was winter time.) He said if she didn't either go out or cut her hair, he was going to hurt her family. This disturbing image finally caught my attention, so I took pictures in her room. The first one you see the perfect outline of a person. The second one I took in the dark. When you look at the dark picture, you think there's a smudge in the middle of the screen, until you look closer. Then you can see it's an evil face. I myself believe in paranormal as I've worked at the Tara and experienced a few things but with skepticism, and this house is right at the bottom of Ohio street. The strangest place I've lived.

Submitted by Aaron, Sharon, Pennsylvania

. . . .

90.
On State Route 60
Zanesville, Ohio

I was beginning to drive out of Zanesville with my friend asleep in the passenger seat. It was about 2:30 or 3 AM, and no other cars were on the highway (State Route 60.) We had just passed the sign that said we were leaving Zanesville and was coming up on the traffic light by the bridge. I noticed that something started from the left side of the highway and was moving right across the road. I went through explanations like "I'm just tired," or "It's just a glare from the light on my windshield. " Then my friend, who I thought was sleeping, said "I think I'm hallucinating. " She was focused forward like I was. I assured her that she was not while continuing to watch this white mass like thing.

It was almost like a cloud, looking smoky, but it never dispersed into the air like you would expect smoke or fog to. It kept a consistent, tight shape (about 6 feet and skinny, almost "person" looking.) It never faltered. It also kept a consistent density. It never thinned out even the slightest like smoke or fog does. It floated about 6 inches from the ground at a steady pace, never speeding up or slowing down across all four lanes of highway. I actually had to slow down because it was so convincing and strange. I felt like I couldn't run into it, so when it made its way to the other side of the road, I sped up and went home. My friend and I never could think or decide what it was, and I can't find anything about similar sightings around the same area. It was by the bridge on 60, north side Zanesville, and it was NOT fog or smoke.

Submitted by Driver, Zanesville, Ohio
. . . .

91.
The Girl Is Emily
Carson, California

All my life I have encountered ghost. I saw my first one when I was four, so I know the feeling of one when one is around. We moved in to a house on Carson Street in Shannon Ranch California about a year ago. Every since we moved in I have felt a presence in the master closet. I cannot go to sleep with the door open. If I do, I wake up feeling someone on my side of the bed staring at me. I have seen a little girl a couple of times, a man, and a woman. Both adults I saw in my bath room and in my closet. The little girl stayed in the left or from what my daughter told me sometimes in her closet.

We were here for about a month and my husband had to work a night shift, so I had the girls sleep with me that night. While we were in bed just about to dose off we heard this loud knock that sounded like it came from the guest room, so I went check it out and found nothing. I went downstairs and check the door and found nothing. Honestly, I felt like I was in some sort of movie. I went back upstairs and told the kids it was just the creaking of the new house we have to get used to, and we went to sleep. About a week later my oldest daughter was talking about a ghost friend she has. She has a wild imagination, so I let her run with it.

A few days after that, I saw this little girl right outside my bedroom. Thinking it was one of the girls I went to see what they needed. I got all the way to the door, and she vanished. I started questioning my daughter about this new friend she made. She told me her name is Emily, and she is the one that made that knocking sound that night, but it did not come from the guest room. She was at the foot of the bed and knocked. I was freaked out for a couple of nights after that.

Submitted by Tra, Carson, California

92.
Feeling Of Being Watched
Dublin, Georgia

I've lived in Dublin all my life. I lived basically my whole life in a house just outside of Dublin. I live near Scotland Road by Bluewater Church. I remember one day when I was about eight, my parents walked outside and left me inside alone. I was tying my shoes when I heard a loud thud beside me. I looked and there was a stress ball that had been on the other side of the room lying there. Needless to say, I finished tying my shoes outside.

I can also remember my mom telling a story of when we first bought the house. I was only six months old at that time. She was inside alone while other friends were in the backyard having a party. As she was walking out, she saw a dark figure wearing a top hat walk out of my room at the end of the house. The figure asked to use the phone to call a friend. Without thinking she pointed to it and walked out. Then she realized and walked back in, and he was gone. She has also felt the covers on her bed tighten up as if somebody had sat on the end of the bed while she was home alone.

As I grew older I enjoyed walking down and crossing Scotland to get to the other side of the road. Every time I would get to the bottom of the hill at the beginning of the road, I would feel like I was being watched from every direction. The feelings only got stronger the darker it got. I have since moved out, but my family still lives there, so please don't try to drop in and check it out. You can walk down the road all you want though, and I guarantee you'll feel a presence. Everybody that I've ever taken down there has said they did without me mentioning it before hand.

Submitted by P, Dublin, Georgia
. . . .

93.
Happy Room
Sheppard Afb, Texas

We currently live on Thor Street. We too have experiences, but it's not negative. When I first moved in I was pregnant, and I was attracted to the back bedroom, the one opposite the master bedroom. (We have the floor plan with the separate washer-dryer closet.) All other rooms were furnished, our master bedroom and my baby's nursery beside our room. However, for some reason all through my pregnancy I wanted to sleep in that room across from us. I felt safe and happy. I did feel watched, and my skin would pop up with goose bumps, but I felt like someone was showing me compassion.

It would just be me in the house while my husband was at work, and I'd go in there to talk about how I felt, and I'd always feel better. My friend walked in one day, although I never told her about the room.

I motioned towards the living room couch, but she went straight to the back bedroom and sat on the floor. The room was still empty. I sat down with her, and it was then I asked her why she wanted to sit here. She said it seemed sunny in there. It was no different than the other rooms, but she felt warm she said. After her other friends would also go directly back there.

When I had my baby he hated his bedroom next to us, so we moved him to the "happy room" (we call it.) He never cries before bed, but I hear him talk and coo, and he goes to sleep on his own. We are a Christian family as well, and we never raise our voice or fight. I guess that helps with the positive energy. Sometimes I do get scared because I feel like I am not alone, but it goes away, and I feel this extreme happiness. I am glad I made that my son's room because everyone likes to sit back there while he plays.

Submitted by Collins, Sheppard Afb, Texas

. . . .

94.
Room 5233
Las Vegas, Nevada

I went to Summerlin on a business trip and stayed in room 5233. After a dinner meeting I decided to go to bed. It was around 10:30 (I know early for Vegas.) I watched a little TV till around 11:00-11:30. I decided to go to sleep, so I turned the TV off and turned off all the lights. At 2:23 am I woke to a glow coming from the bathroom, and I thought to myself, "nice! They have night lights in the bathroom.) I went to the bathroom, and the light on the swing mirror was lit. Now I did not turn it on, and it was for sure off when I went to bed. I turned it off and went to sleep.

The next morning there was nothing unusual. I came back that evening, and my buddy and I decided to drive home, so I packed my bag and said to the room " it's all yours" as I left the room. I turned and walked down the hall. In my left ear as loud as can be I hear a whistle like "whhhhoo" and a soft slap to my left ear. Oh man, goose bumps. I got to my buddy's room and told him the story, and we went back to the spot to see if maybe there was an AC vent that may have turned on as I walked by but no. We got back to the room, got our bags, and left.

I had a bag on wheels that I pulled in the hall. I felt like the bag was being held back as I walked, and I was dragging it down the hall. My buddy even noticed it as well. As we approached the elevator, the bag just released like nothing happened. We got to the valet, and my buddy had to tell them what happened. They said straight faced "what floor?" I told "the fifth," and they said they have heard of stuff on the sixth floor, but not much on the fifth floor.

Submitted by Ralph, Las Vegas, Nevada

. . . .

95.
On The 4th Floor
Guthrie, Oklahoma

My daughters and I spent last Friday night in a room on the 4th floor of the H.I. Express. We were nearly asleep, when my daughter who was in bed nearest the window, started to speak. The moment she started talking, my youngest daughter, who was in bed nearest the bathroom sat up, startled, and said "did anyone just see that white shadow walk across the room?" I was a little disturbed, but I didn't want her to freak out. I said it was just the lights from the highway. She was convinced she had heard something though. She had heard steps and seen a white figure head toward the bathroom. She thought it was her sister until her sister started talking from her bed. I kept changing the subject, and we finally fell asleep.

The next morning I decided I would bring it all up again after we left the room. My daughters were taking a long time to get ready, and I was bored waiting on them, so I went to the window, opened the curtains wide, and let the sunshine in. I then said "I was going to wait until later to say this, but I think we had a ghost in here last night!" Right then, the hotel telephone rang! My oldest daughter jumped and yelled. I was surprised, and then frightened a little when I went to answer. There was no one on the phone. It had only rung once. I said "Let's get out of this room."

Submitted by Lori, Guthrie, Oklahoma
. . . .

96.
Standing Guard
Lorain, Ohio

I lived on W. 22nd Street in Lorain, Ohio in a home that my grandfather built as he built homes for all his children. Well I've always been a hustler, mowing lawns, etc to make money. I saw what I know was a ghost soldier at the Old Charleston Cemetery on 5th and 6th Streets as it sits between these two streets. I must have been around nine to ten years old at the time, but I had the nearby customers who lived in the mini mansions, and I'd mowed their lawns every week. Well, there was a young man dressed in very old military attire that I'd see each time I came to start my mowing in the neighborhood that is very affluent. He seemed to like me, so to me he was my friend, and I liked him. He was always there standing or rather floating at least 3 feet in the air holding an old musket, and his civil war uniform was greyish. He was actually standing guard at the old cemetery, and he was very young, I'd say about 15 years old.

I've gone back and still do through the years and have taken my wife with me to show her where he stood which was on the 6th Street side next to an old home. Some of the graves were moved and carried to other cemeteries. Since then I haven't seen him anymore. I miss him because I always thought of him as my friend because he'd always appear when I got there to start my mowing. He never said a word, but he had a pleasant appearance on his face, almost a little smile.

Submitted by Aaron, Lorain, Ohio
. . . .

97.
From The Open Closet
Lexington, South Carolina

Around thirty years ago my husband and I built our home on property which has been in his family since the 1850s, complete with family cemetery located on neighboring property about a quarter mile down the road. Even before our home was completed, I sometimes felt the presence of someone watching me, and there have been many odd happenings over the years. We have had doors swinging open, the sound of someone walking through the room, and so on.

There was a one and only time that I ever saw a tangible "ghost" or whatever it was. I woke up in the middle of the night and saw a little girl dressed in white standing beside the bed. I leaned up on my elbow and tried to speak to her, but was too shocked to form words. She looked alarmed that I could see her, and she retreated into the open closet and disappeared among the clothes. Just as she disappeared, I heard my son who was about three years old at the time coming down the stairs. He and I have always had a very close emotional connection, and I think he sensed that I was disturbed. Weird stuff. Needless to say, I NEVER go to sleep with the closet door open any more.

Submitted by Donnak, Lexington, South Carolina

. . . .

98.

The Industrial Park

North Attleboro, Massachusetts

Last month I moved from Kentucky to North Attleboro, MA. Originally I got a job in Providence, but the company closed down right before we were moving, so I took a job in North Attleboro. My company is located in the industrial park, and I work the graveyard shift doing manufacturing. I don't know anything about the area. On my break around two thirty am I like to take a walk to get some fresh air and exercise. I like how peaceful it is and the weather is now nice, but twice I've seen a ghost. I NEVER believed in ghosts, and sorry to say I never took people who saw them seriously, thinking they were just seeing things.

However, twice when I've walked by a location in the industrial park I've seen a man. I can't get a clear picture of him since it's always been from about thirty feet away, but he's looked me straight in the eyes and both times said "He did it" before fading away. I have no idea what that means, and both times I've run back to the building, daylights scared out of me. I haven't told a soul. People will think I'm crazy and I don't even really know anyone here since I've just moved. I needed to get this off my chest and share and ask if anyone else had experiences in the industrial park. I always think of ghosts as old and wearing old clothes, but this man was wearing modern looking clothes, stuff we'd wear today. I'm so scared and feel like a big baby.

Submitted by Mark, North Attleboro, Massachusetts

. . . .

99.
Cat's Crying
Vallejo, California

I was a young boy growing up in Vallejo in the early 50s, living on Broadway, at the west end of Springs Road. Across the street from our house (though no longer there, since replaced in late 50s when a curved street was put in to connect the south end of Broadway into Alameda Street) was a block of storefront businesses. Right across the street was McConologue's Model Market. There was a passageway between a couple of the buildings just to the north of Springs Road that was kind of spooky. Anyway, when I was about five or six years old, I was kept home with some sort of fever or illness for about a week.

One day, looking out across Broadway toward the street in front of these buildings, I saw what I was sure was the body of a kitten that must have been struck in the street. It was there for a day or two, then gone. Later on, after 1956 when I started going to Vallejo Jr. High and had to walk to school past this spot, I would often hear the plaintive cry of a cat. A few times when I would hear this, I would walk into the passageway, looking to see if I could find the cat. Although I could hear it, I'd never see any sign of it. But I sure do remember to feeling of dread I would get the further down that walkway I would go. I sure was glad when they tore those buildings down because I never heard that cat's crying again.

Submitted by Steve, Vallejo, California
. . . .

100.
Old Convent
Belcourt, North Dakota

I live in some brand new apartments that was built on what used to be a nun's convent. Well the first incident happened when my kids and I were home alone. I was sitting on the couch; my 5-year-old and 10-year-old were playing games on the laptop, and they were lying on the floor. My 5-year-old turned around; she was not looking at me but past me, and she said "Mama, there's a man with a black hat behind you!" I hesitated to look, so I turned my head slowly to look, and my daughter laughed, "he ducked down, and he's hiding from you. "

The second time happened when we were eating supper. My 10-year-old son rubbed his eyes, and said "I don't know if my eyes are playing tricks on me, but there is a shadow behind you. " I became curious, looked up some pictures of old convents, and as I was scrolling just as my daughter walked by, she pointed at a picture of a minister in a black hat and said "there he is!" Well my son walked by also and pointed at a picture of a nun and said that is what the shadow was shaped like. I immediately got the apartment blessed because one day I was messing with the black and white effect on my camera using my cell; I took a picture of my arm because there was a constant icy hot feeling on my arms. I contacted a paranormal group shortly after, but I haven't gotten any responses yet. The picture has since convinced me there are spirits here.

Submitted by JaeF, Belcourt, North Dakota

. . . .

101.
Haunting Spectacle
Columbus, Indiana

My brother and his wife have a one-year-old child, and over the course of the last year we've seen some paranormal oddities. I was hanging out with my brother at his home and had to use the restroom. The nearest one was around the baby's room. For a while now it was haunted, such events have been so frightening that my nephew would be paralyzed by fear. As I went to the bathroom, I approached it with caution. I was one who always held an eye towards the possibility of the paranormal. Knowing there could be a ghost in the residence certainly interested me, and such events I have witnessed I have full belief in the paranormal. I was hesitant to use the restroom and had questioned the placement of my brother's shower curtain.

For some odd reason I had felt it was supposed to be open, but it was closed. I questioned my brother to this and had him come over to inspect. We both peered in to look at the bathroom. I felt foolish being startled by literally nothing. I stood behind my brother one hand on the left wall and the other on his shoulder. He had his arm inside the bathroom out of my view, and the other against the door frame. What happened next was enough to solidify my views on a great many things. At first it was silent, but then I heard a click echo, the doorknob to my nephew's room had turned. In slow and steady form the door opened with only the slightest creek, and I had alerted my brother. His first action was to question my hand in the door opening, to which I insisted that my hands did not move to the door. We both heard the click, and watching the door open was a bit of a shock that immediately stole my attention. Paranormal was in my opinion solidified. It brings to wonder what other areas of North Vernon, Indiana might hold the haunting spectacle.

Submitted by Bob, Columbus, Indiana

102.
Lining Up At An Inn
Lenoir City, Tennessee

My wife and I were going from our home in Alabama to Pigeon Forge Tenn. On vacation. We had not made reservations; we were just going to rent a room after we got to Pigeon Forge. As usual there were several functions going on, i.e. car shows and such, so we could not find a room anywhere after we arrived. We decided to go back out of town, and the first place we could find a room we would stop, stay the night, and go back to Pigeon Forge the next day. We drove to Lenoir City and found the Inn of Lenoir. We went in and rented a room, and the hotel clerk took us all the way back to an old part of the Inn. The lighting was dark. The walls in the room were dark. The room was small with a TV on the wall and a bathroom with two full size beds with metal head and foot boards, and the carpet was old and the room was musty smelling. The atmosphere was very eerie. My wife turned the TV on and left it on.

It was getting late and my wife and I were very tired, so we went to bed. I never sleep well and it takes a long time for me to go to sleep, especially in a strange place. I had been lying in bed for a period of time when I saw transparent looking people in all periods of dress start lining up just inside the door. As they would come inside the door in line, the one in front of the line would stop a few feet away and then rush over to the bed where I lay. Then he or she and would slow down and look at me just like one would look at a person that was in a casket. Then as they would reach the foot of the bed, they would rush back over to the door and exit. This went on all night. I thought I had been dreaming until the morning.

I told my wife about my experience when we got up to leave. My wife looked at me and said "if it were a dream, then we both had the same dream because the same thing happened to me. " We turned on the TV and Kenneth Copeland was on. We watched him while we were getting ready to leave, and we left the TV on with Kenneth Copeland preaching. My wife was so distraught over what had happened that she didn't take time to put makeup on before we left. We were in a big hurry to leave the Inn of Lenoir. Whether a dream we both experienced or spirits checking us out, I really can't say, but it was an experience I will never forget.

Submitted by Grover, Lenoir City, Tennessee

. . . .

103.
Not Alone
Austin, Texas

I've been living on South Lamar for a little over two years. I've moved from apartment to apartment. I like the area for the reason that it's close to work for my girl and I. There is something odd about living in this area. Every apartment I move into gets worse as far as noises and visions. Our first apartment since day one had an odd smell and weird feeling. I say odd smell because out of nowhere the smell of rotting meat would fill the room. We are both vegetarians, so that makes it kind of odd. Now other times the smell of roses and incense would fill the room.

One night my stereo turned on at full blast at around 3am. The stereo is not an alarm radio. I woke up one night to the shower water running at 4am. At our second apartment I was fixing breakfast for my girl and I while she was in the shower. She was in the shower when she heard the sink water go off then the toilet flush, and she thought I was sharing the restroom. She also said the hot water was extremely hot, and she could not turn the cold water on. When she tried to open the restroom door it was stuck. It was as if the door was locked from the outside. When she screamed out for me I went over and opened the door. Nothing was wrong. The door had been unlocked. Her car keys that morning were not on the dresser where she normally leaves them.

I dropped her off at work, and when I came home to the apartment the dishwasher was on. No one had set it to wash. There were only a few dishes in there, and when I shut it off the garbage disposal went off. Something was messing with us. The on and off switch didn't turn it off, and I could hear some kind of metal fork or spoon in the disposal. I got the apartment maintenance man to come check it out and explained all the strange things going on. He shut off the breaker to get to the garbage disposal. He said something was jamming it. He then reached into the disposal and

172

pulled out a set of car keys. As soon as he pulled his hand out the disposal went off and a kitchen light was flickering on and off. He explained that it was impossible for electricity to be flowing with the breaker off. We went back to look at the breaker, and it was back to the on position. He was just lucky his hand didn't get torn up. We talked a bit, and he told me these apartments had been built over an old cemetery. He was convinced what'd been happening was the works of supernatural entities. We moved out shortly after.

We started having problems getting along, and now we're separated for the time being. We're hoping things will get better with time away for a bit. I thought living alone would help us grow closer, but it's driving me nuts. I'm still having similar issues as far as stuff being moved around, lights turning off and on, doors shutting on their own, windows being open, and water running on its own. Only this time I feel someone or something moving around in my bed, someone following me around the apartment, or someone always watching me. I guess I'm not alone after all.

Submitted by Sam, Austin, Texas

. . . .

104.
A Little Boy By The Pond
Athol, Massachusetts

I do not know what to believe anymore when it comes to ghost sightings or not. I had something happen to me years ago down here in MA. It freaked me out, and the only person I told was my husband who like myself was a huge skeptic of all of this stuff. Years back in the mid 1990s I was walking at a high school down here trying to get back in shape. I would walk the track that is located just up from a pond by about 160 feet. During the summer months there was summer school at this high school, so some of the younger kids had recess time, and they were playing on a field closer to the school baseball game. Teachers were around the area. I was alone on the track walking fast with my headphone on listening to morning conservative talk radio out of Boston. I feel so weird even telling this story. I feel like I sound nuts.

I saw this very young boy, closer to a four-year-old all of a sudden walking along the chain linked fence that separated the school field and area from where the land drops down to the beach below and the pond. However, all of the chained link area is huge bush growth, extremely high and thick. This little boy was blonde and had on shorts, and a little short sleeved shirt that was stripped. I knew he was too young to go down the stairs near the pond. I was on the other side of the track, and began to yell to him "hey! Don't go down there. Listen to me." I was screaming at him. He never looked at me once, ever! He proceeded to walk down the cement stairs onto the beach area. I was in full blown running. I was now going to be right on his heals. I ran down those stairs so fast, looked to the right and left, and straight across to the water, like maybe he went into the water. He could have been drowning. I then looked along the bushes. They are so thick; you cannot get into them. He disappeared! I thought I lost my mind when I saw him as clear as day, and then he was gone in a second after hitting the first couple of stairs.

174

I am a runner from the 80s. I did not lose this kid. He disappeared! I was so freaked out by this experience. I never went back. When my nephew got older, I told him about this. He is a very smart guy, and he did not know what to make of this either. We come from a family of skeptics. He knows I am not nuts! I would never make anything like this up. I brought my nephew to Ireland for his high school graduation gift, and then for his college gift. The second time over, we got a chance to get into the most haunted castle in Ireland called Leap Castle in County Offaly. You cannot just make a reservation. You can only call when you are over there and hope that particular day the owner will let you in. His name is Sean Ryan, which just happens to be one of our Irish family names of Ireland. After our tour in the castle we sat down with Sean and only one other couple from the U. S. and had a great long talk about the hauntings in this castle.

This was the only time I opened up in front of strangers about what happened at that track at that high school in the summer of 1997 in MA. I told Sean Ryan exactly what I just told you, and he said to me "did this little boy ever look at you?" I said NO. He said "you saw a ghost of a child that does this all the time, but will only appear to certain people. " I asked him "why me?" He said "because they know who to appear to... Who will care. " I have been so bothered about this that I went to the Fire Department near this high school, and asked one of the firemen working that day if he knew of any boy that had ever drowned in that pond behind the high school in the past 80 years. He did not know. I do not know who to ask. I think this child drowned in that pond. This is what he did before he died.

When I got home that day from the track I described his little shirt like a shirt boys would have worn back in the 30s or 40s. I am very artistic and creative, so I remember detail! I would say he was three and half to four years old. I can still see it in my head today. Like I said, I would not go back! I am very practical, and this did not make any sense, when I ran down those stairs, and could not find him. I then ran back up the stairs and went to my Jeep. I drove home to tell my husband what had just happened. I do not have any photos, just my story of what happened to me that day back in 1997.

Submitted by Suzan, Athol, Massachusetts

. . . .

105.
Red Brick House
Saint George, Utah

In the heart of downtown St. George there is something of a non-descript two-story red brick house. Built in the 1950s, the home has seen a lot of living, and apparently dying within as occupants have come and gone, imparting something of themselves to the home like a recording, a memory kept forever in the brick and mortar.

Our experience with the home began in the early 1970s when we moved to St. George from another small town in Utah. There was always an odd feeling that seemed to permeate the walls. Not of something frightening, but a feeling of something "other" that occupied the same sphere as you. Certain rooms felt alive, as if there were person or persons within that would disappear as soon as you entered the room. As children, my brother and I would hear movement in the basement and see fleeting glimpses of someone moving, always just out of reach. Shadows and whispers from the stairwell or closets were a common occurrence.

My brother vividly remembers looking out the window of the front door. It was the kind with the wavy glass that made the view slightly blurry. On that occasion he happened to see the face of an old man staring at him through the glass, wide eyed as though noticing the child on the living room floor for the first time. The face had no body attached to it, turning its gaze as if firmly pressed against the glass.

On another occasion I myself was awakened from sleep one night for reasons still unknown to me. I remember seeing a hunched figure, luminous, walking down the dimly lit hallway toward the kitchen as it passed by my bedroom door with arms swinging casually at its side. I assumed it was my father, but when I called him my father soon walked from their own bedroom across from ours dispelling any thought that the figure had been my dad. We moved not long thereafter. I've always been curious if any of the subsequent residents have experienced similar encounters.

Submitted by Me, Saint George, Utah

. . . .

106.
In The Apartment
Dekalb, Illinois

What place isn't haunted in DeKalb, right? I was living on Regent Drive and that place had lots of strange happenings. We would always hear footsteps. Doors would close and open on their own. There was once a huge gust of wind that came from nowhere and knocked out the attic door in our roommate's room. You always knew someone was standing over you and watching you. One time I was sitting on the couch, and I saw my purse topple off the table. I understand how gravity works, but the purse was entirely on the table. No part of the purse was hanging off the table.

I ended up moving out to live with another friend who needed a roommate. Since I already graduated, I didn't know if I was going to stay in DeKalb. I did, and I went to visit my good friend who still lived in our old place. They locked off my bedroom, so that my two old roommates couldn't sneak anyone in. She and I were in her room when the door to my old room started rattling as if someone were trying to get out. The windows were closed, and no one has been in that room since I moved out.

All three of us would text each other to ask if the other was home because you would always hear someone walking around the apartment. One time I was in my room with a friend after I got home from work. My roommate's door was shut, so I assumed she was sleeping.

My friend and I were hanging out when I heard my roommate open her door and leave the apartment. I felt bad because I thought I woke her up. I opened my door, and her door was wide open. I texted her to ask her if she had left because I was being too loud. She said that she hasn't been at our place since 7:00 pm. This incident happened around midnight.

That's just skimming the surface. I wish I could find information about it, but I never have any luck.

Submitted by Nina, Dekalb, Illinois

. . . .

107.
Unwelcome in Maybee
Maybee, Michigan

I grew up outside of Belleville in the 50s and 60s. I had my own paranormal experiences by our home on Belleville Road near Ecorse as well as in the Tyler Road Cemetery. Since I was young, I heard numerous people talk about Maybee that the "town wasn't right," "the people who live there are weird," or "too many strange things happen there. " Maybee is out of the way, and I rode through the village just a few times when I was young. Nothing out of the ordinary happened. I moved from Michigan in the 70s and went back over these past holidays for a visit. I got together with old high school friends one evening at a bar for beers. Out of nowhere, one of the guys said he had a strange thing happen in Maybee the other day. My ears perked up as he began to tell the story.

He is a building contractor and drove to Maybee to look at a renovation job. He had a young helper with him who he recently hired and had just moved to the area. As they approached the village, the young man made a comment how uneasy he felt and the place "was creeping him out. " It was broad daylight, and Maybee looked like any other small town. My friend thought the guy was just being weird. Somehow my friend got turned around and could not find the home they were looking for. The helper started to panic. My friend looked over at him, and he was sweating and pleading to leave the area. My friend asked him "what was wrong?" The guy just went on about how scared he was. He said "I could never work here" and "this place is bad. "

My friend thought the guy was on drugs or something and left without finding the house and drove back to Ann Arbor. When they got far enough away from Maybee, the helper calmed down and admitted he sometimes sees ghosts, and once in great awhile when he enters a house, business, or in this case a small town, he gets an overwhelming feeling of dread or danger and have to leave. My friend is a very practical person, but when I heard the story I told him about the stories of Maybee and his helper was probably feeling something there. Then I checked this sight and noticed the sightings by others, and yes, I believe the young man was unwelcome in Maybee that day.

Submitted by James, Maybee, Michigan

. . . .

108.
Still Here
Zanesville, Ohio

I live in a house that was haunted. I had it blessed and asked the spirits to leave, and I believe they did. My eight-year-old daughter and I moved in this house when I married my first husband. I have seen a jar that was on the counter lid come off, fly into the middle of the kitchen, and drop. I put a candle arrangement on the mantle in our living room. Before I got back into the kitchen the candle arrangement was disassembled and laying on the floor. The TV would turn on and off by itself. The rocking chair would rock with nobody in it. My daughter is very sensitive to ghosts. She would see them, and they talked to her. She is 31years old now. She still sees ghosts now and then. She doesn't speak with them because she says they can be annoying. She also is afraid if she does talk with them, her gift will get stronger and draw more spirits to her. I guess she is what you call a medium, though an unwilling one.

My husband had never seen anything here, so I told it "Why don't you bother him?" Well, it did. I went to bed before him, about thirty minutes later he beat it upstairs to our bedroom. He wanted to know if I shook him awake in the family room and told him to go to bed. It was not me. My husband passed away a few years ago. I have caught glimpses of him a couple of times and felt his touch. He also tossed a picture of my cat out on the floor several feet from the table it sat on. He used to get aggravated at my ornery cat. I had surgery a year after he died. I could feel him sitting on my hospital bed with me. My father-in-law saw him in his hospital room the day before he died. It was like my husband returned to help his father into the afterlife. It made me happy to know he is still near us because I still love him very much.

Submitted by Lynn, Zanesville, Ohio

. . . .

109.
Grapevine Ghost
Bakersfield, California

Late one rainy cold night my mom my sister and I were driving the Grapevine north back to Bakersfield. Now it was around 1 am and we stopped at a rest area. No one was there no other cars trucks or anything.

We all got out and should have stayed together but went 3different ways to restrooms. Pitch dark wild freezing wind and drenching rain. Well after we regrouped at the car we all had an eerie story to tell.

My sister told us of a handsome young man dressed in black that crossed her path. He smiled and seemed almost perfect. Mom said I saw him and he smiled tilted his head and opened his arms as if he knew her.

I also saw him in another part of the restroom same thing. He beckoned to me as if he knew me. As we stayed in the locked car and talked it was realized that we all saw him at the exact same time in 3 different places.

He was beautiful and had long dark hair and eyes. So we got the courage up to walk back and find him but he had just vanished. He seemed good not scary. Something very different about this guy. However I prefer not to visit desolate reststops now.

Submitted by Haley, Bakersfield, California

. . . .

110.
Warning
Pickens, South Carolina

The house on Greenville hwy, one that was painted white that was wood frame and owned by the family across the street who lived on a farm. We rented that house in the 1990s and it has since been bulldozed; we saw last year. Some strange things like a noise of someone walking and actual footprints in dust in one small room happened. Two large black dogs were seen running out of the fog behind a hay bale but disappeared when they reached the chain link fence. An Indian with a bow and arrow was also seen behind a hay bale early one morning in the fog. It faded away. Two of the other rental houses that were about 75 years old down the highway on the other side burned down due to faulty kerosene heaters the owner told us.

Two other rental houses were remodeled, and the owner's son moved into one. Now it is bulldozed. There was a two-story very old house about to fall down in the middle of the woods across the street from where we lived in the last house. Cats with no tails would come from there. We found children's toys buried next to the last cement step at the back porch. There was an old wooden chest there that had decayed into the soil. It had semi-precious stones in it. One morning there was a rainbow, and it appeared to end in that very backyard. We will never forget that either.

The houses were rental houses for a long time. They all had fireplaces. I found a stewardess's metal pin in ours. I saw a man seated in our upholstered chair through the doorway of the small room late one night when the kerosene heater was found to be running out of fuel. I had woken up and turned it off. He was a blonde man and disappeared. He was warning me I think. None of the houses are standing now on that side of the highway. Now a new house has been built where we used to live on that lot.

Submitted by Sharon, Pickens, South Carolina

111.
In The Middle Of Nowhere
Ubly, Michigan

My girlfriend and I rent a small home in Ubly, and something or some things are living in it or around it too. One time I was in our bedroom alone, and she was on the couch in the living room. Well apparently she saw a dark shadowy man with an old style hat come walking out of the room I was in. She never said anything about it until a few weeks later when I was awakened by what felt like a hand sliding between my legs as I lay on my stomach asleep. Initially I thought it was her hand, but I woke and realized she wasn't in any position to come from beneath me.

Then one morning I slept in and was awakened by my cat and dog locked in the bathroom crying and scratching to get out. Then another night we both heard a girl's voice outside our window. It was around 3:00 am, and if you're in Ubly you know it's in the middle of nowhere. We hopped up to check on her son and found nothing. Kids have complained about stuffed animals falling over without being touched. One morning I woke up to what sounded to be five or six people knocking on the wall from the next bedroom. We shut all the doors when we leave and somehow on occasion stuffed animals will be scattered throughout the house.

Submitted by Ben and Loretta, Ubly, Michigan

. . . .

112.
Jeremy
Oklahoma City, Oklahoma

I work at a Subway on Hefner and Rockwell. I have worked there for almost a full year now, and the last few months some crazy things have happened. I wasn't the person who discovered the Ghost. To be honest I don't know who discovered it. I will only write the experiences I had or have seen.

One day I was working the drive-through, and it was about the end of our daily lunch rush. The stations that hold our different items for sale has a metal covering, and while I was making a sandwich, out of the corner of my eye I saw something move in the reflection of a part of the metal lining. I looked into the metal and saw a shadowed figure come up and walk behind me to what would be the front lines (the front of the store where we are making customers sandwiches.) When I turned to see who it was no one was there.

Another time again when I was working drive-through, out of the corner of my eye I thought I saw a certain male co-worker walk past me going into the back of the store. Turning to look again I saw nothing. The strange thing is that everyone who has encountered this "Ghost" at the time all thought it was the same said male co-worker as before.

Now for the strangest. I wasn't there, but we have it on camera. A squeeze bottle for our sauces flew off of the shelf holding it diagonally into the dishwasher, all by itself. The dishwasher was not running at the time, and no one was around it. Another strange occurrence is when we are closing we will hear someone laughing in the lobby, and no one will be there. There will also be times when the bread cabinet's doors will open themselves.

At first it creeped all of us out, but we have gotten used to the strange things, and now we blame all the strange little things on the ghost. We call him Jeremy.

Submitted by Jane, Oklahoma City, Oklahoma

. . . .

113.
I Don't Believe
Highland, Michigan

It's funny. I don't believe in ghosts, and I still don't to be honest, but I've always loved a good ghost story and very much into horror novels and movies since I was a child in the early 80s. I've seen and heard many odd things over the years; most notable years would be 1985-1988, 1995-1999, and 1999-2003, and now 2003-present. Each of those time periods represent a different house I've lived in along with the duration of my residence. The really interesting experiences all took place in those two last time periods, but it's the one I currently live in that freaks me out the most.

Since I started living here I've noticed a few oddities and the what not and usually brushed them off as my eyes playing tricks on me or my body reacting to the mass quantities of caffeine I usually ingest. A few times while making a snack in the kitchen I got feelings of something walking past me towards the bathroom. That particular phenomenon has happened about four times.

The usual odd noises and smells often happen and still do. A few of the noises are loud, and they sound like pipes and fans working overtime. The house has thin walls, so I still feel these occurrences in house noises causing feelings of dread with noise combinations. I've seen my cat looking at the darkness of the bathroom quite a few times and even spotted her walking along the rim of the tub and purring as if she's being petted by something I couldn't see. These odd instances have happened in the last 3-4 months for the record.

It's the recent activity that bothers me to no end and actually gives me the shivers as the sightings are completely random and usually occur before the morning really gets going. On four separate occasions I've seen these rather tall and thin columns of light

189

moving in one direction for about 1-2 seconds and then disappear as fast as I see them. Three of those sightings have occurred in the kitchen area and one in my room while I was lying in my bed. That last one was a bit freaky as it was right next to my bed and at the corner of my eye.

The most recent sighting of this entity was yesterday morning at around 7am in the kitchen. I turned the lights on, walked back to my room, and walked back only to see that thing appear and disappear right next to the refrigerator. I get my hair standing up and chills on my back as I type this up. I had to put some music on while typing this to offset some of that feeling.

Submitted by BJ, Highland, Michigan

. . . .

114.
Still Happening
Buncombe, Illinois

I have been a resident of Buncombe most of my life. I lived in three separate houses, one about a half mile outside of town and two in town. Things happened in all of them. I had feelings of being watched, hearing noises and voices, and things being moved. I've experienced a lot growing up. After eleven years my husband and I decided to buy a house in Buncombe, so we would be closer to our family. When we started remodeling tools would go missing, or if you set something down just for a minute, it would be moved somewhere else.

After I moved in my granddaughter's toys would come on by themselves. Lights would flash on and off. We would hear running through the house in the middle of the night, banging in the attic, and doors closing opening and locking on their own. We had handprint on the walls as well as 12-inch-footprints under the living room furniture.

My husband saw a little girl about right years old one morning (he's not so skeptic anymore.) They stared at each other for a minute. Then he said she disappeared right in front of him. I used to get bruises on my inner thighs. Some looked like fingerprints, bite marks, and scratches. Some looked like I had been beaten with a bat. We also had our voices imitated, and things were thrown. My granddaughter has two imaginary friends (Opal and Prince.) It got so bad I had investigators come about two years ago to try to help, but it made it worse for awhile. It's calmed downed quite a bit this past year. Things still happen, just not as bad.

Submitted by Samantha, Buncombe, Illinois
. . . .

115.
She Is In The Closet
Greens Fork, Indiana

I had moved into a small country house in Greens Fork on State Road 38 in the summer. Across from the Greens Fork Flea Market coming in from a big city in South Florida, the quietness of the country was an adjustment. The odd sounds we would sometimes hear, we chalked up to being solely our adjusting to the country life. The home had a very creepy feeling in only one part of the house. It was an area where there was an oddly placed closet. The room adjacent to it, which was my son's room, was always cold. My son never slept in that room. He would always say it was just too cold and weird, so he would sleep in the family room on the pull out couch. It was only in this particular room that we would feel an eerie sense that someone or something was watching you. I always felt it was female.

My boyfriend eventually set up his art studio in this room. He then confided in me one night that he would feel that someone was in the room with him. He is a huge skeptic and never talked about these sorts of things. He would feel uneasy in that room. I had never told him about the weirdness my son and I would feel in that part of the house. He had confirmed that night, that there could be something paranormal in my house.

I had learned to ignore the creepiness until one day. I saw it. We eventually moved out, and it was during our transition from moving that the activity in the house increased. Doors would open and shut. Objects would be misplaced then found again in odd places. There were always shadows moving around. It always felt like there was lots of movement. It was as if the presence was upset that we were moving away. It never felt menacing, just creepy. During the last few days, I was scanning the house for left over trash from the move and/or items left behind. When I approached the closet and closed the door, while sliding the closet

192

shut, I saw a half apparition of a woman sort of following the movement of the closet as I shut it. I closed it immediately. I said I was sorry for leaving and hope she finds her way to GOD. I ran out of that house and do not care to ever go back.

Submitted by Julia, Greens Fork, Indiana

. . . .

116.
The Husband
Bolingbrook, Illinois

We purchased our home about eleven years ago. A previous owner who had been widowed had done her best the fix the place up for sale but had done a rather shoddy job of it. My husband and I constantly made jokes about what a crappy job this woman had done. We didn't realize that her husband had died in the home. Once while we were in the master bath, we were complaining about the workmanship, and a metal wall hanging flew off the wall and barely missed hitting my husband in the back of the head.

The television on the lower level will sometimes turn itself off, or the garage door will go up by itself. We've had the wiring checked, and there's nothing wrong with it. At times when I'm home alone, I'll be cleaning or something I'll hear someone call my name. I know there's no one at home besides me. It's a little unnerving. On occasion I'll smell cigarette smoke very strong, but I'm the only one who smells it. I'm sure it's the husband of the woman who previously owned the house.

Submitted by Rosie, Bolingbrook, Illinois

. . . .

117.
A Mass Murder Location
Fort Valley, Georgia

I lived in this home that was the location of a mass murder. We didn't know it at the time we moved in, but we all noticed weird and unusual stuff happening here. It has a very creepy vibe to the land that all the trailers and houses were on. There were two houses in particular that caught my attention. At the bottom of the hill there was an old white house. It was really cold, and you get chills and goose bumps walking into it or anywhere near it.

I decided to venture in one day with my then-boyfriend. We took out our cell phones and hit record. We started asking questions, and upon listening to the answers I felt a stinging sensation on my back. Upon checking over it, there were three scratch marks across my lower back. When I walked out of the house I looked at the log cabin that was right next to it, and there was a full body apparition staring at me from the window. I turned and called for my boyfriend, but when I turned back it was gone. There's been so much activity we were forced to leave.

Submitted by Chi, Fort Valley, Georgia

. . . .

118.
Their Previous Home
Destrehan, Louisiana

We live in Ormond in Destrehan. Before we bought our home an older man lived and died there. My family renovated the house and moved in. About 15 years ago when I still lived at home I would wake up in the middle of the night and see a man's figure standing in the doorway of my bedroom. What was so odd was I never felt scared, but I am the type of person who would freak out easily.

My mother would say she could hear hushed voices talking at night and would think someone was on the phone in another room. When she would check on everyone, the entire family was sound asleep, but she could still hear the voices.

One night my mom had just looked around for the voices only to find everyone asleep, but as she left one bedroom and walked into the hall, she saw just the legs of someone go around the corner. She ran to catch up, but no one was there.

Several people in our family and visitors to our house have felt someone sit down on the edge of the bed while they were sleeping or before they fell asleep at night. People have also told us they suddenly felt a gentle pressure on their foot or leg, as if someone was holding it over the covers.

My dad has never believed us, but recently he was lying in bed facing my mom in the pitch black. They were not asleep, but they were awake talking. Suddenly he heard a noise behind him next to the bed, and when he went to roll over he felt someone touch his arm. He freaked out and turned on the lights, but no one was there.

My husband says he always feels nervous or like someone is watching him when we are there, especially when it's quiet or you are alone. One night my husband and I were there alone, and both were having strange feelings. When we left and went home we started hearing weird noises in our house, and our dog kept staring at the ceiling and into the foyer and growling. We thought maybe the spirit followed us home, so we told it nicely to leave, and the noises stopped.

We luckily all agree that the spirit(s) are nice and are more just visiting us in their previous home.

Submitted by Elizabeth, Destrehan, Louisiana

. . . .

119.
He Was In The Basement
Sterling Heights, Michigan

I had a relative that lived in a house on Maplecrest Road in Sterling Heights. I visited there often as a kid. I had great memories there but also very bad. Well the bad stemmed from a ghost that haunted the home. We were told by a neighbor that the man that owned the home before my relative had killed himself in the garage. I can go on and on with stories, but I will tell you just one that really sticks with me.

We were playing hide and seek. I picked the basement, bad idea. Well, while hiding behind the furnace in the dark I felt someone touch my shoulder. Of course I went running and yelling, and everyone followed. We all ran to one of the bedrooms where we all hid shaking. My cousin then dared me to open the door and look to see if he was there. Well, like a young and dumb kid I accepted his dare. My older cousin decided not to let me go alone, so I went first, and she held on to my shirt. I led us up the hall towards the living room. In shock and disbelief there he was sitting on the couch staring out the window. He had a worn brown suit. We were both frozen and could not move. He then turned his head and stared right at us. I was about to soil my pants. We ran back for the room, and I called my brother to come get me. I was so scared to go through the living room. I jumped out the bedroom window.

Needless to say my uncle finally moved. From that period forward this house always seems to be for sale. I feel for anyone that lives there. Anyone out there know the house I am talking about?

Submitted by S, Sterling Heights, Michigan

. . . .

120.
Little Bones
Plymouth, Ohio

My husband and I were out on Father's Day just driving around and, I spotted this house that was empty. I told him to stop; I wanted to get out and look in the windows. I fell totally in love with the home. I had to have it. He called the number that was on the sign, and believe me or not they came over and let us go through the house. I fell even more in love with the house. We ended up getting the house by October of that same year. Come January we started to fix the house up. We started with opening up the second floor. We put up a beautiful oak railing, but on the other side of the steps is another way to go down them. We took that door off to open it up and noticed that the third step up had hinges on it. I thought what on earth, I got a crowbar and hammer and had to pry the step up. Someone had nailed the step down.

When I finally got it up and under the step was a brown paper bag. It looked like it had been there a long time. I opened the bag, and inside were small bones. Me liking things like this I didn't think anything of it. I told the kids that it was probably a family pet and didn't think about it anymore. I cleaned out all the dirt that was under the steps and found out that the crawl space went all the way under the steps. I decided to put the hinges back on the steps the way it was to begin with. I never thought anything more about it. We continued working on other rooms in the house.

We opened up the third floor and made it into a big game room for the kids. It was then when all the noise and weird things started happening. We would get a lot of bats inside the house. You would think that they would be on the third floor, but no they were on the first floor. I had a real good friend staying with me, and it scared the hell out of her. She always heard people walking when she went to bed. She never wanted to come down the stairs when nobody was up.

Anyway, back to fixing up the attic; we could tell that there was some kind of fire up there, but nobody ever told us about it. We put up new boards, paneled the ceiling, and painted everything white. If you look up at the chimney up there, you can still see that there was some kind of fire up there. To shorten up this story, it was not until we moved out that people were asking how we stayed there so long. People were telling us that the people that had lived there way before us had a daughter, and she got pregnant and was not married. She had lost the baby when she was in her last trimester there in the house. They never took the girl to the hospital, nor did they ever call the police. They didn't want anyone to know. People say they buried the baby in the house.

To this day I always wonder if the bones I found under the steps were the baby. People also said that the reason they turned the house into an apartment house, upstairs and downstairs, was so that when the daughter got older they didn't want her out of their sight. It was also said that when they moved out the grown daughter moved with them.

I don't know who bought the house next, but whoever did left it as an apartment house. The family that lived in the downstairs was playing with one of those Ouija boards, and that is when the fire started, maybe whatever they called up are the ones that we heard walking around. I will also tell you this; when you drive by the house and look in the third floor window on a dark night, you can see a face.

A lot of bad things always happened whenever we did work on the house. When we hired people to paint the outside one of the men fell off the roof. He was OK but did hurt his back and leg. We also had gravel put in. When the guy dumped the load, for some reason the truck bed went back up again and tore of some of the roof where all the windows are on that side of the house. Also,

200

in the small backyard is a little hill; the kids would ride their toys down that hill. You will see the remains of stone steps, people say they lead to hell.

Submitted by Mikey, Plymouth, Ohio

. . . .

121.
Cherry Road
Oswego, Illinois

My friend and I decided to go for a drive down Cherry Road one night. We were both bored and were at the White Castle drive-in looking for something to do. We were both curious about the paranormal, so we at first decided to go to the old Copley Hospital, but soon knocked that idea out of our heads just because we weren't totally sure where it was at.

We had heard all the stories about Cherry Road so figured why not. Whenever we go for drives we always hit Cherry anyways, so we knew it pretty well. As soon as we neared the curve of the road, I pulled out my iPhone and started snapping pictures. Looking through them I didn't notice anything (I was driving, so I wasn't paying attention to my phone really.)

I handed the phone off to my friend who I was with. He looked at the pictures, and then we saw it. At first we didn't really know what it was, and as we looked at the picture more began to appear. Our first thought was that it was the girl who died, and we were seeing her spirit.

We sent it off to a friend who then took a better look at it. We realized it was very evil. It wasn't nice and weird things started happening after that. Thankfully I'm a strong believer in the Lord, so a lot of praying helped out a lot. Needless to say, we NEVER go down that road anymore. You couldn't pay me to do it.

Before this happened we were with our other friend one night, and we drove through a small patch of fog on Cherry Road right at the curve, and she said she felt something go through her. I then read and heard that at that curve someone had buried someone they murdered. Hence the reason evil lurks there. Feel bad for anyone else that tries messing with it. I couldn't sleep for a long time afterwards.

Submitted by Liz, Oswego, Illinois

. . . .

122.
A Child, A Teen, And A Grown Version
Carlsbad, California

I was followed by a ghost lady for a few years. I woke up one morning around 3 am. I sat up, looked at the clock, wiped my eyes, and looked around. As I looked forward, a lady stood at the end of the bed with a beat up dress and her hair covering her face. I let out a yell and put the covers over my head. I told my family members what I had seen, and of course no one believed until strange things occurred to them which was exactly what happened. I was about to graduate RBV when I first told the story and I remember people saying "she wants to tell you something. " My first reaction was "then you spend the night and ask her yourself. "

A few weeks after I graduated my mom moved in, so since we rented out my godmother's garage I told her I'd sleep on the floor and told her to take my bed. At around the same time I awoke to the sound of a woman crying and crying right next to me. For some reason I thought it was my mom, so I sat up and asked her "mom what's wrong?" She kept crying. I asked her again "mom what's wrong?" No answer again. The woman never once looked up. That was when I had a feeling it wasn't my mother I was talking to. Without looking I extended my hand towards the bed and squeezed my mom's foot. She moved it quick and said "don't tickle my feet. "

I looked back at the weeping woman and turned the opposite direction and lay there listening to her sobbing 'til I fell asleep. I told my story to many who all suggested that this woman wanted to tell me something. I then decided to buy a tape for my recorder and went around the whole house asking questions such as "what did you want to tell me? What is your name?" The next morning an EVP attempt failed due to the tape on the cassette had been cut. Eventually we moved to La Cascada Apartments.

One morning I parked by the Samoan church, and as I was walking to the pad, I heard the sound of little feet running, and it was a little girl wearing the same dress running from car to car ducking and giggling. At 2 am I knew she wasn't a normal little girl, so I booked it and quickly went inside. Just to make sure I wasn't tripping I opened the door, and she kept running going from one tree to the other hiding and giggling. I woke up my gramma and told her I got followed by a little girl. My gramma said "she wants to play with you. " I said "but I don't, so what do I do?" She told me what to do, so I went outside. I told her I couldn't play because I was tired, but she could play with the curtains that that was her spot and no one would bother her. She disappeared and I closed the door relieved she was gone. To my surprise the curtains began gently moving as if someone was running their fingers across them.

The whole rest of the morning I kept checking and the curtains kept moving until around 7 am. I saw her one more time after that incident, but she was in her teenage years. She was making a hand gesture indicating for me to follow her, but I refused, and she was gone. Strange happenings occurred, but that's a whole other story. I haven't seen her since. I looked into it, and I found out there is an actual demon who comes to people in all 3 stages a child, a teen, and a grown version.

Now I wonder was she a ghost trying to reveal some sort of secret or was it a demon trying to gain my trust, so it could take me? Till this day I still question why it was me she wanted. I guess some things were meant to remain unsolved.

Submitted by Will, Carlsbad, California

. . . .

11829330R00115

Printed in Great Britain
by Amazon.co.uk, Ltd.,
Marston Gate.